A BOY FOR ALL SEASONS

6/96

Best Wishes

Tim &

BF(

A
BOY
FOR
ALL
SEASONS

TIM WIBKING

FOXHAVEN PRESS
Franklin, TN

ISBN 0-9651747-0-0
LIBRARY OF CONGRESS CATALOG CARD NUMBER 96-96248

FOXHAVEN PRESS
P.O. BOX 436
FRANKLIN, TENNESSEE 37065-0436

COVER PHOTOGRAPH BY JANET DITTUS
PRINTED BY POLLOCK PRINTERS, NASHVILLE, TN

THIS BOOK IS DEDICATED
TO THE MEMORY
OF
NATHAN

~ ~ ~

CONTENTS

INTRODUCTION

Once upon a time, a princess kissed a frog who was transformed into a prince. While I am not a prince, I was very similar to a frog, or rather its cousin the toad. I was a lawyer with a small but growing practice. My marriage to Janet, a physician with a thriving practice, brought many challenges and blessings. Little did I realize that when our son Ben was born on Father's Day 1991, he would become both my greatest blessing and challenge.

Over the next two years, I moved my practice to our house, stopped taking new clients, and phased out my existing base. Using common and financial sense we had agreed that I would stay home to raise our son.

Time passed and the year 1994 arrived. As parents learn, if they do not already know, time does not carry the same weight with children as it does with adults. I felt my time slipping away into pointlessness until one day, upon hearing my feelings, an acquaintence suggested I write about my unconventional parenting experiences. My interest was piqued, and I found myself collecting bits of conversation with my son. For about a year, I felt a strange gestational glow with my embryonic ideas. And so it was that I was enveloped in the magical timelessness of my son's third year.

In this time and place, Ben and I learned the art of

companionship. Talking, and listening, and playing. I had yet to put a single word on paper, or more precisely, open a file on my computer. Fate stepped in to give me a push. Once while watching *Mr. Rogers' Neighborhood*, the popular children's television program, Ben asked if Mr. Rogers could visit him. Not one to disappoint my son, I suggested we could at least write him a letter. And at Ben's insistence, I helped him write a letter to his television friend. As if to affirm the magic of our time, we received a warm reply of encouragement, and from it grew these conversations with a three year old...truly this father's gift.

Tim Wibking
Franklin, Tennessee
1996

SUMMER

The kind of man who thinks that helping with the dishes is beneath him will also think that helping with the baby is beneath him, and then he certainly is not going to be a very successful father.

-Eleanor Roosevelt

SUMMER

HAPPY BIRTHDAY
***

Nags Head, North Carolina was an isolated peaceful vacation spot - in 1975. We shopped at R.V. Cahoon's, the grocery store and general store, near Whalebone Junction. When we ate out, it was at Sam and Omie's, a rustic place with sawdust on the floor that began serving breakfast for the fishermen at 5 a.m.

Times change, and Nags Head is not the sleepy undeveloped beach hamlet of my youth. R.V. Cahoon's is still there, but so are hundreds of other shopping places. Sam and Omie have left their restaurant to new owners who have swept away the trademark sawdust and added potted plants.

But our family, having embraced it once, still loves Nags Head and we cling to it as we age, and return again every few years bringing now our own children. We are fond of traditions, and children, and grow them with care.

We chose June for our visits, though we have had to find a newer rental cottage. The older place we stayed at for so many years deteriorated rapidly after the owner became too old, or rather infirm, to maintain it, and the rental company didn't keep it up. They couldn't have known the wonders of childhood that had occurred within its walls, else why would they let it fade and rot?

The last time we were in Nags Head we rented a house

with a crow's nest for viewing the sunrise on the ocean and sunset on the sound. To the south you could see the Bodie Island lighthouse, an especially wonderful view at night as its light swept a full circle through the blackness.

The new house had promise with its crow's nest. Inside, there was a guestbook in which one previous occupant described her awakening during a thunderstorm when lightning struck and set the crow's nest ablaze. A place with a brief but already fabled history was the kind I wanted for my family's budding traditions.

And so we returned in 1994: my parents, my brother and three sisters, their spouses and children, and my wife Janet and our son Ben. In the last week of spring we traveled from our homes in Tennessee by various routes and managed to all converge on the Outer Banks at roughly the same time and place.

It was middle June, the 16th, Ben's third birthday, and we celebrated it at the beach. He loved the birthday parties he attended for others. He was puzzled now for some reason, maybe timid, or self-conscious about the attention he received on his own special day. He knew everyone, we were all family. Still, Ben seemed simply overwhelmed. Nanny, as my mother was now known in the family, started talking, telling her stories, and Ben focused on her and visibly relaxed.

"I just like the icing," Ben said. "You eat the cake."

Ben scooped the icing onto his spoon leaving the cake on the plate. Ben pushed his paper plate toward me. I obliged by finishing my son's piece of cake.

"Here, have your own piece," Nanny said.

"No thanks, I've got plenty to finish," I told her as Janet shoveled some of her own cake toward me.

"See," I said, as I barely had time to open my mouth to receive the fork full of cake.

"Feed me, too, Mom," Ben said.

"Like father, like son," Janet said.

"When I was growing up," said Nanny, "all we had on our birthday was cake and grape juice."

I smiled knowing that Nanny was about to hold sway over the family gathering with her well-honed storytelling ability.

"And you walked five miles to school through the winter blizzards," said my older brother Ron, or Unc' Bro as Ben called him.

Ron and his wife Cathy had three children who were Ben's closest cousins as well as good friends. Matt was 12, Katie was 10, and Lyndy was soon to be 6. Ben loved to visit and play with the kiddles, as he called his three cousins. Ben was an only child and he unleashed his full energy when he was with them.

"Well, that's right, and I'll get to that story, but first let me finish the details of my birthdays. Did you know," Nanny said to Ben, "that I had to make my own cake from scratch?"

"Scratch?" Ben asked and laughed, "What's scratch?"

Everybody laughed.

"That's the ingredients," Nanny continued.

"He doesn't know what ingredients are," Papa said.

My father had become known as Papa when he became a grandfather. In fact, my own grandfather - Nanny's father - was called Papa. Probably, I would be Papa someday and after me, Ben would be in his turn. Traditions ran deep in our family. Many sayings and ways of living were passed down from generation to generation, but only to a select few was passed the gift of gab - the oral tradition of passing family lore and memories like a runner passing a baton in a relay race.

Nanny had this gift. I did not, and I did not know whether Ben possessed it, though I believed some would rub off on him. He appreciated the stories, and that was enough for this season, the beginning of many seasons.

Papa and I helped Cathy and Janet clean up the birthday litter. In our family it wasn't unusual for men to help with the household chores. Papa had shared most of the cooking and other household chores with Nanny when I was a child.

Papa was an only child, and served in the Navy in the Pacific at the end of World War II on a supply ship. His chief duty was as a cook where he acquired and honed his kitchen skills. Later, Papa became a college professor, and Nanny a nurse. With both working outside the home and raising five children, they had to share lots of household duties to stay afloat.

I took that as part of the tradition passed down to my

generation. Though I could have rejected it, I didn't. Instead I had a sense of familiarity to my newly assumed role of full-time, stay-at-home dad.

Still, I was not oblivious to the stereotyped responses of some. I wanted more than once to ask whether it was rudeness or stupidity that prompted a disparaging remark about my decision to be a full-time dad, but couldn't bring myself to say the words with a straight face - even when a neighbor made light of my chosen role, saying, "That's what we use to call a wimp when we were growing up."

Rude or stupid? A little of both, I think.

Society hasn't given me much help. My job doesn't have a simple moniker, but instead a convolution of words and hyphens, such as, house-husband, stay-at-home-dad, Mr. Mom. I can't even say I'm a full-time dad without drawing cock-eyed expressions and raised eyebrows.

And so I simply do, as my family has always done for generations, that which needs to be done. Somebody has to do it. For everything and everyone, there is a season...and a reason. If you believe children are the future, and an honor to the past, then you too know a child, like my son Ben, who needs you.

And so, surrounded by family and vacation wonder, Ben celebrated his third birthday at the beach in Nags Head.

"I'm finished now," said Ben as he pushed away his plate and slipped down onto the floor. "Let's go build a sandcastle."

COFFEE AND THE AMERICAN DREAM
***

Stone walls dating from the early 1800s lined the rolling countryside in the county where we lived, just outside Nashville. Horses and cattle still grazed the pastures, though sub-divisions had sprouted all around.

Our house was nestled, really, at the edge of a forest, right at the foot of one of the rolling hills. The lights glowed from the house to this thick black woodsy backdrop. And the light was held there, suspended in the air, glowing a golden syrupy hue.

Back from the beach, it was now officially summer. It was also the summer I began recording the conversations Ben and I shared each day. They would be simple and elegant, I imagined. Sophisticated. Philosophical. Probing. Enlightening. Frustrating. Joking. Experiences in human relations and character development.

Ben was growing in ways too profound for me to fathom. I thought my own son "brilliant", of course, but not in ways of just intelligence. Ben had a brilliance of spirit. I didn't want him to lose that - or to forget.

"What was your great-grandfather?" I asked Ben.

Ben usually wouldn't respond to these new topics immediately but waited to hear the comment several times for context comparisons. And then only when he was interested.

Ben and I were sitting in our screened patio, cups and coffee set.

"How's your coffee?" I asked of Ben's mostly milk concoction.

"Good. And yours?" he replied.

"Really fine."

Ben 'ah-ed' to show his pleasure.

The kitchen phone rang and I stepped just inside the patio door to answer it.

It was a former client who was in need of an ear.

"I've been moved from my apartment - it's in the projects. It was leaking and unfit to live in."

"How much damage was done to your personal property?"

"Well, it was water damaged for a while. They want me to pay moving expenses."

"I could refer you to another attorney who could help," I said.

"Well, thank you," she said as I gave her the name and number. "But, I think, I just need to tell them I spoke to you. I don't think they'll call you back."

It was at times like this that I felt a pang of guilt over my decision to abate my law practice.

"You can tell anybody you want that you talked to me," I said.

"Thank you."

"How are you gettin' along?" I asked.

"Well, jus' makin' it day to day. Rely on the Lord."

"Maybe things'll start looking up," I said.

"Oh yes, things'll get better," she replied. "Thanks." She hung up.

"Doesn't sound much like the American Dream," I said out loud to myself after hanging up.

"What have you been doing?" I asked Ben as I rejoined him on the patio.

"Who was on the phone?" he responded.

"An older woman who needed some help."

"What's an older person?" Ben asked.

"Like your great-grandfather," I said.

"What was your great-grandfather?"

"I'm not sure. He supposedly came over from Germany in the 1800s to somewhere like Missouri or Illinois. But we don't know for sure. He had a baptismal certificate from a Lutheran church in the early 1900s written in German, so I suppose it's true. In any case, he was part of historical human migration."

"But why did he come?" I pondered as I took a big gulp of coffee.

"For the American Dream." Ben piped up loud and clear.

I struggled to contain my mouthful of coffee.

"Good coffee," Ben added.

***

FAMILY REUNION

***

North of Franklin lay Nashville, and further still up I-65 was Bowling Green, Kentucky in the heart of the Bluegrass State. Of Nanny's family, the most lived in Kentucky and the rest in nearby satellite states. We drove north of Bowling Green, then east on the Cumberland Parkway past the toll booths at Glasgow, Edmonton, Columbia, and off at the Jamestown/Russell Springs exit.

Every year for the past ten years, we made this trip and spent a three-day weekend on the grounds of Lake Cumberland State Park at the old Pumpkin Creek lodge. The lodge was built of rough hewn timbers and logs that would have made the original pioneers through the Cumberland Gap beam with pride if not envy. About 50 relatives filled the lodge to capacity. It was the closest accommodation that adequately met our needs and placed us within a winding 20 mile drive to the old homeplace, where Nanny, her siblings and her parents had lived since 1918. Nanny's mother and father were known to me as Mama and Papa Holladay. Papa Holladay lived to age 91, being born in 1876. Mama, or simply 'Holladay' to me and my brothers and sisters, died in mid-July 1984 when she was two weeks shy of her 97th birthday. That's why we chose the reunion for the last weekend in July - it was closest to her birthday, July 28th.

Nanny was raised in a large, by today's standards, farm family. There had been nine children in all - three boys and six girls, all born in that farmhouse or nearby. Nanny and her twin sister Ruby were next to youngest. The Holladay family lived on 100 acres of rolling, partly wooded, creek crossed, spring fed, and fertile Adair County farmland.

"Tell me about the olden days," Ben said.

Nanny and her sisters sat in the lodge drinking coffee and talking. All the sisters and one brother lived on. The sisters always turned out for the reunion, and sometimes the brother. The children generally made it as well, but the grandchildren, especially those moving into their late teens strayed and stayed away. It was a fairly expected phenomenon. Those older family members at the lodge were able to share a memory that the younger ones hadn't experienced, and the younger ones who came to Pumpkin Creek Lodge made memories of that place and of us and each other, but absorbed only the watered-down version of the original homeplace memories.

Hearing someone with the gift of gab spin stories about the olden days was mesmerizing. Nanny told Ben about wading through Runnels Creek, swimming the Blue Hole, fishing for bluegill, collecting eggs to sell at Montpelier (the general store and post office), walking to Pleasant Hill country day school (the one room school Nanny and her siblings had attended), and using the wood burning stove for heating and cooking. She started to tell about the famous Halloween outing to Ghost Coffee's house when Ben interrupted.

"No Nanny, I heard that," Ben said. "Tell me about the real olden days."

I entered the room during the storytelling, and took a seat in the great room where the aunts, or 'the sisters' as they were called, were visiting and storytelling. I looked around the room admiring the knotty pine paneling. And I listened to the warm tones of the voices.

As I listened to the adults, I closed my eyes. Memories of long ago were awakened. I recalled times as a young boy, I had listened with my brother and sisters through an upstairs bedroom floor grate, late night, to adult conversations in Granny Holladay's kitchen.

The highlight of the weekend was the family play. Bro encouraged the children to prepare and act the roles. Aunt Ang wrote the script and directed the scenes. Papa and Bro made the set which included a mural of the homeplace on an 8'x 8' sheet. Ben announced the beginning.

"Hi-de-ho, neighbors," Ben said before taking his place in the audience. The play retold the quirky events of the family. It was highly appreciated. Afterwards, punch and cookies were provided just like a 'real' post-theater reception.

After a Friday evening and Saturday spent visiting and eating and playing, the families loaded cars Sunday morning for the trips home, heading out toward all points on the compass. Some had golfed, others shopped in

Russell Springs, a few visited the new cappucino cafe in Columbia, but most had come to talk and walk the ground of their youth, and remark on the changes of people and places.

As we drove on the parkway and paid at the first tollbooth, Ben said, "I wish we didn't have to leave everybody."

"But everybody is leaving and going to their homes, Ben," I said.

"I mean, I wish everybody didn't have to leave," Ben explained.

And I was about to say that everybody had to leave and they would visit again next year, but paused in thought. I knew that leaving was what people did and there were no guarantees that there would be a next year, and so I said, "Me too, Ben, me too."

***

WATCHING MR. ROGERS

***

"Is Mr. McFeely coming today?" asked Ben.

The day had rolled by like the great dark thunderclouds that sailed across the sky, hurtled by the southwest wind. Fatigue set in as Ben fought off another nap. The late afternoon hours were spent watching *Mr. Rogers' Neighborhood*.

We were both fans and knew all the characters.

One time, Mr. McFeely, a favorite character, brought over a dead bird, and Mr. Rogers spent the show talking about death. Things just got stranger after that.

"Why is that bird dead? Why did Mr. McFeely bring a dead bird to Mr. Rogers?" Ben could sure ask the questions.

But, I wondered silently, why did Mr. McFeely bring that bird in that condition? So they could talk about death? I didn't like to think about it because when I did I thought about sick kids, like Ben's distant cousin Nathan who had been receiving treatment for a brain tumor for most of his life. He was about Ben's age.

Of course, Ben and I wondered about a lot of things. And some we talked about.

"Let's sit and chat," is what Ben's cousin Lyndy would say, but she was six, an age of considerable social talents, I had noticed.

But Ben was three, and his conversations were based on his activities. His conversation skills ran to imperatives and questions. Ben fixed his bright blue eyes on me. This look during Mr. Rogers' show meant: "Get the trolley."

I left the room and returned with the music box trolley. I wound it and gave it to Ben. Ben pushed the button and the Tony Bennett song about San Francisco played. On television, Mr. Roger's trolley chugged around the bend to the land of make-believe.

There was a knock at the back door. It was Jack, our neighbor who had been retired for several years and now puttered around the home. Jack and his wife Dorothy were good neighbors. They were easy-going, liked Ben, and collected mail when vacations took us out of town. Ben liked to mow grass with Jack, who had a John Deere riding mulch mower. Ben had a Little Tykes bubble mower. Once a week, at least, they mowed their separate yards. Ben would stop to watch Jack ride round and round.

"Gimme five," said Jack holding his palm out to Ben. Ben placed his small hand on Jack's and smiled.

"You be Mr. Rogers," said Ben.

"We're watching Mr. Rogers," I explained.

"I'll be Mr. McFeely," said Ben, and then, "Speedy delivery!"

"Goodness! He hasn't changed in 20 years," smiled Jack commenting on Mr. Rogers' appearance. Jack's hair was white and sparse. His skin was softly aged, his eyes tired but clear.

"You're my neighbor," announced Ben.

"That's right," agreed Jack, "And that's a rare commodity nowadays."

"What's a rare 'modity?" asked Ben.

Jack's eyes widened as he looked to me for help. Ben turned back to the show.

"I grew up about 12 miles from here in a farming community called Centenary," Jack said to me. "You never heard of it. It's gone now. Just a few implements rusting in the fields." He grew quiet as his memories transported him many years into the past.

"My grandfather - he raised me - taught me to take care of implements, not leave them rusting in the fields like they are now. First you cleaned them and oiled them if they needed it and then you put them in the barn."

"Put them in the barn," Ben echoed.

"We had neighbors." Jack continued, "When somebody got sick, everybody knew and came by to help bring in the crops or whatever was needed. People knew everything about each other, even what you had for breakfast!"

I listened intently and offered, "Things today are made to be thrown away, but good neighbors..."

"...are few and far between," finished Jack.

On television, Mr. McFeely was mowing his lawn in fast motion. Mr. McFeely was showing Mr. Rogers a home movie.

Ben stood up and walked over to where my guitar

leaned against the wall. It looked like the biggest guitar in the world next to Ben. He held it like a bass and strummed all the strings with his little hand.

Ben sang, "Mr. McFeely mowing his lawn, Mr. McFeely mowing his lawn."

"Wo, wo, wo," added Jack tapping his foot.

"Mr. McFeely mowing his grass," yelled Ben.

"Mr. McFeely run out of gas," I said.

"Wo, wo, wo."

"Fill, fill, fill," sang Ben, "Mr. McFeely mowing his lawn."

And then he stopped, put down the guitar, and crawled back into his chair.

All three of us burst into applause.

"I'm so glad we had this chance to get together," said Mr. Rogers, but we didn't hear. We were still laughing and clapping.

***

FINAL TOUCHES

***

"Get the big saw," said Ben.

The jigsaw was well out of Ben's reach, at the back of the shelf. I brought it to the workbench, blade removed.

"Plug it in," said Ben. I started the saw.

Ben backed away as he always did, "It's too loud."

I turned it off and unplugged the jigsaw.

"Let's use another saw," I suggested.

Ben had his safety goggles, or eye protection as we called them, in place and adroitly held his small dull handsaw in his left hand.

"Won't cut this wood," he said.

"What do you want to saw?" I asked.

Ben pointed to a two by four.

"What do you want to cut it for?"

"I want to build a house," smiled Ben.

I remembered when Papa let Ben mark lines on bits of wood with his metal measuring tape and then helped hammer them into his screened-in porch. It was natural then that Ben would want to move on to home construction.

"I'll get my big hand saw," I said. "Now where do you want to cut?"

Ben pointed to a spot about two inches from the end. Ben held the saw with me as I cut.

"And here," he directed me.

I was starting to sweat. Ben agreed that four pieces would suffice.

"Now, what are you gonna do with these pieces?" I asked.

"They're the final touches." Ben beamed.

We got sand paper and smoothed off the splinter wannabes. Ben carried the blocks out of the garage to the six-foot-long wooden airplane that Papa had built for him.

"This is our house. This is Nanny and Papa's house. This is Cathy's house. This is...," Ben recited as he walked.

"We could paint the final touches," I suggested.

"Okay, get some paint."

We had tubes of acrylic water based paints and brushes for just such a project. The wing of the plane served as a palette for the red, blue and yellow colors. A plastic cup was filled with water, brushes dipped and loaded.

"Wipe it off," Ben complained, fingertips all red. I rubbed his small fingers with my own.

"We'll wash off when we finish. Just don't rub them on your clothes. Clothes are harder to clean."

To my surprise, Ben followed this guidance.

We painted the blocks red and made yellow marks for the windows and doors. Ben let me finish while he finger-painted parts of the airplane.

"I'm making dots," he said.

When the houses were dry, Ben carried them inside where the next connection appeared to him.

"Let's go to the sandbox," Ben said. So we went onto the back porch to the sandbox.

"I'm gonna bury them," Ben announced. And he did. Then he dug them out.

Then we smoothed roads and made a subdivision. The bulldozer and backhoe were fast at work.

"Get some water," said Ben and so I filled a pitcher. "I'm gonna make a pond."

The water was quickly absorbed.

"Get more water," Ben said.

"Let's use these molds to hold the water," I suggested. "Smooth the sand close like this and you can put the houses around them."

Ben tried to wash his houses but I convinced him to stop when we saw the paint coming off.

"I'll make a car wash," said Ben as he dipped his cars in the pools.

Later that night, Ben and I soaked in the tub.

"Float me," said Ben.

He leaned back supported by my hands. He let his ears submerge with his face looking out the window at the night sky. Ben jabbered to himself enjoying the sounds distorted through the water.

"What do you see?" I asked him.

"Stars," he replied. And then he asked, "What are stars?"

"They're big places, far away. That's why they look so small."

"Can we go there? Way up there?" Ben held his arms out to reach and fly.

"We could go in a rocket ship and blast off," I said.

"We'll light it and blast off," echoed Ben. "Can we build it?"

"Maybe we'll need a spaceship too," I said. "Because stars are so far away."

"Can we go there?" repeated Ben.

"In our imagination we can go. We can pretend."

"We can fly in our airplane," said Ben. "I made dots on it today."

I recalled Ben's finger painting. Was he painting dots to represent the stars?

Ben held his arms wide and I swayed him gently from side to side.

"Brrrun," said Ben as he blasted off.

***

BEDTIME STORIES
***

"Tell me a story," said Ben as he lay in his toddler bed partly covered with a blanket from Nanny and surrounded by his stuffed animal friends.

There was Stephi bear, Eddie Bauer dog, Marahute the eagle and his favorite Mouseybear. Mouseybear was his lifelong companion and best buddy who wore plaid pants and Christmas-lightbulb decorated ribbon suspenders over his eight-inch high frame.

"Okay," I said, as I always did. "How 'bout Pete the bulldozer?"

"How 'bout another one, a different story."

"Okay, you cover up and hold Mouseybear, and I'll tell you a new one."

Ben hugged his buddy close and waited with eyes open wide in the paleness of the nightlight.

"In a house in the woods Mouseybear was busy in the kitchen."

"Why was he busy in the kitchen?" Ben asked.

"He was cooking food," I improvised.

"Why was he cooking food?"

"He was hungry."

"Why was he hungry?"

"Well, I'll tell you," I said.

I tucked him in with Mouseybear held gently in his

hands. I recalled the uncertainty upon admitting Mouseybear to our household about whether it was a mouse or bear. It was small and white, but also had facial features resembling a teddy bear.

"Mouseybear got a frying pan out of the cupboard. Then he got eggs from the refrigerator," I said. "Just then Benjaminbear came into the kitchen and started to help."

Ben smiled faintly as he imagined the friends in the kitchen.

"Benbear held the spatula while Mouseybear cracked the eggs and poured them into the pan. 'Don't touch the pan, it's hot,' said Benjaminbear. Mouseybear listened because his buddy knew about such things. Benjamin stirred the eggs to make scrambled eggs. He was careful with the spatula so he wouldn't spill the eggs on the stove and make a mess."

"Mousey didn't make a mistake," Ben interjected.

"That's right. He was careful. Papa bear entered and said, 'Smells great. How about some bacon, too?' So Papa microwaved some bacon. It smelled great. Everybody ate some but before the second helping Papa suggested they go for a walk in the woods which they did. While they were out walking, their cousin Lyndy stopped by. She had short straight black hair but they called her Lyndylocks anyway. She sat in Mousey's chair and broke it all to pieces. She ate Ben's bacon and eggs and went to sleep in Papa's bed."

"Then all the bears came back. Mousey said,

'Somebody's broken my chair all to pieces.' So Benbear glued it back together."

"Why did he glue it back together?" asked Ben, sleepily.

"Because it was broken," I responded.

"Why was it broken?"

"Because Lyndy sat in it."

"Why did she sit in it?"

"She made a mistake."

I waited. Ben remained quiet. I continued the story.

"Ben said, 'somebody's eaten all my bacon and eggs!' So Papa cooked more food and they all ate 'til they were full. Then Papa went to bed for a nap, called the others and said, 'Look who's sleeping in my bed.' It was Lyndylocks."

"They gathered around and nudged her awake. At first, she yawned, then awoke with a startle. Once she recognized her friends, she moved over so Papa and Ben and Mousey could crawl in too. They all settled in, pulled up the blankies and went to sleep."

I quietly tucked in Ben, who was now fast asleep.

***

SILLY AS A GOOSE

***

"I'm hot as a lizard," said Ben.

He had been playing in the sand pile with his construction equipment. It was one of those hotter than normal mid-September afternoons. The kind that Nanny would call 'burny'. Ben's face reddened easily from play and exertion, tiny beads of sweat popping up on his nose, just like Janet. I considered genetics, then offered bottled water which Ben accepted and gulped thirstily.

"Want a snack?" I asked.

"Sure," Ben said, nodding once for emphasis.

We brushed off sandy feet and shorts before entering the house. Ben liked to rub his feet on the coarse bristles of the welcome mat, and he eyed me to ensure I followed suit.

Inside Ben dragged his bar stool to the sink, crawled up on the counter, put his feet up, and turned on a light stream of water. While Ben washed and cooled off, I looked around the kitchen for snacks.

"Want a brown snack?" That was our name for Little Debbie Fudge Rounds, a sort of chocolate sandwich cake.

"Sure."

"How about raisins?"

"Sure."

"Apples?"

No answer. I got one from the bin in the refrigerator. I peeled and sliced it. I dried Ben's hands and feet and set him on the counter which extended between the breakfast table and the kitchen. We ate quietly enjoying the respite from the work and heat.

"Cathy says these are good with milk," said Ben, as he ate his fudge round.

I wondered if Ben's aunt Cathy really said that as I poured a glass of milk.

"Can I have a Swiss Miss?" Ben liked the chocolate pudding of that name.

"Are you sure?"

"I am."

When we were nearly finished with the Swiss Miss, Ben said, "I'm full."

"Just one more bite," I urged.

"I'm full as a tick," said Ben. Ben always picked up on the sayings passed down the family tree by Nanny.

"I'm full as a lizard," I laughed, waiting for correction.

"No, full as a tick, and hot as a lizard," explained Ben.

"You're silly as a goose," I laughed.

"Silly as a goose," echoed Ben.

"Let's hurry and straighten up now," I said. "Then we can take a bath."

"Let's hurry," agreed Ben. "Quick as a wink."

We cleaned up and went upstairs for a bath. I ran the

water while Ben pulled off his clothes. As I turned the water down to a trickle, Ben appeared around the corner.

"I'm naked as a jaybird," he chuckled.

And he sprinted off for the ritual chase scene preceeding his baths.

***

FALL

Some of my best friends are children. In fact, all of
my best friends are children.

-J.D. Salinger

PRESCHOOL

***

"Is he gonna be my friend?" asked Ben.

Janet had just told Ben about another boy who would be in his preschool.

"Tomorrow you'll be going to school. And he'll be your friend and you'll have lots of friends," she continued. "And it'll be fun."

"It'll be fun," he agreed.

Ben had heard stories from Lyndy, who was in first grade, and he had seen Mr. Rogers visiting kindergarten and first grade. Now he would go to school, too. I wondered if he dreamed about the trolley-school bus, or little chairs and tables, or stories and toys. What did someone so small, so young, imagine about such things. I felt nervous and sentimental. I didn't remember being three. What were the important things that mattered then?

The next morning Janet and Nanny and Papa, who had arrived for the big day, set the upbeat mood.

"This is your sandwich. You have turkey," Janet said. "And here's some Goldfish crackers and chips. And here's a cookie for dessert. In your thermos you have Kool-aid."

"Do you like your lunchbox?" asked Nanny.

"I do," said Ben.

He wore overalls and a long-sleeved knit shirt - clothes he had picked out himself. He wore Stride Rite shoes with velcro straps and black socks.

"Like Papa," he announced.

We all drove to preschool which was inside a big church on the corner. Papa carried the video camera and recorded the historic event.

"Bye," said Nanny as she stopped outside the door. The door opened and the camera recorded as Ben walked inside holding his lunchbox and Mouseybear.

"May I help you?" The director greeted us at the door and ushered us to the classroom. Inside were tables and chairs just Ben's size. His teacher showed Ben where to place his bag. Ben set Mouseybear beside his bag, turned for a hug, and walked off to begin his play. There were two others already exploring the toys in the room. Quietly, we left the room.

At home, we were ready for a call to come get Ben because he couldn't stop crying because he missed us. But the call didn't come because Ben didn't cry. He was having fun. Of course, we didn't know this but we hoped it was so. We would have to wait.

"Did you have fun at preschool?" asked Janet later that night with a touch of apprehension in her voice.

"I did," said Ben, "Can I go back, right now?"

***

GOING HOME

***

One day every week, Ben and I drove to Nanny and Papa's house. The drive seemed interminable even though it was only an hour on I-24 to Clarksville, Tennessee.

"Find some music," Ben said and I punched the scan button until I found something I recognized, usually from the sixties, late seventies or early eighties.

Sometimes Ben would say, "That one, turn it louder, " and we would drive, not speaking, listening to Aaron Neville or Carly Simon.

Sometimes Ben would say, "Not that one, some other music," and I would punch another button.

This time Ben said, "Sing about Nanny and Papa," and so I made up a traveling song.

"We're going to Nanny and Papa's, Hi ho the derry-o, we're going to Nanny and Papa's."

And Ben sang, "Where is Papa's? Where is Nanny's? Ding, dong, ding."

We read signs on the trucks, too.

"What means wide turns?" Ben asked. Regardless of the answer Ben repeated the question.

The drive took us along I-24 through rolling hills covered with oaks and maples, poplars and sumacs. In September and October, the trees brightened into beautiful golds and reds and browns.

Eventually the interstate took us to Clarksville, the town northwest of Nashville where I had grown up. A few minutes after exiting the interstate, we turned down the final curving lane to our destination.

"Ah, beautiful road, " Ben said. "Trees and grass."

And indeed the last stretch was beautifully laid down through a hilly forest that greeted us every time, and we rolled down the car windows as we rode quietly through the neighborhood begun in the 1960s.

The children I knew had all grown up and left now. But their faces rose up in my mind with each visit like pieces of a puzzle which I had long ago squirreled away.

"I'll come around and get you out," I said as we parked in the driveway. Before I could do so, Nanny and Papa were out the backdoor, ever smiling to greet Ben with the warmth that all children should receive.

"Let's mow some grass or till some dirt," said Ben to Papa. And so they did with Papa leading the way and Ben trotting alongside.

Inside there was always the fresh pot of coffee ready for me and some treat like cinnamon rolls or country ham and biscuits. Food seemed to be omnipresent. Mashed potatoes, green beans, corn and casseroles were available constantly. Nanny kept Hershey's Kisses and Reese's Cups in a cabinet drawer easily within reach of the grandchildren though, surprisingly, they rarely overindulged.

Outside Ben and Papa followed the machine around the yard and after a few minutes they turned it off, satisfied that some attention had been given to the earth.

Ben remembered the brands of lawnmowers he came across. He recognized Toro, John Deere, Kubota, Craftsman and Snapper. He relished visits to Sears just to sit on the riding mowers on display.

Papa went to Loew's, a large home improvement store, allegedly on a daily basis. Ben gladly rode along. Papa showed Ben the machines and tools and lumber which were needed for the great airplane and porch projects, as well as for the final touches. Papa helped Ben sit on the lawnmowers on display.

What was the association between the toys Ben saw at Service Merchandise, Wal-Mart, Target, Toys-R-Us and the lawn mowers? Whatever it was, Ben subconsciously made that association.

He made the connection with heavy equipment too. He could name Caterpillar, Case, Bomag and Ingersoll-Rand on the bulldozers, back-hoes, drum rollers and asphalt spreaders. These machines he saw on his videos, and on road and home construction sites, and in the toy versions in the sand pile in Nanny and Papa's backyard.

Upon the return from Lowe's, Ben joined his cousins, who had come by after school. Ben got in the sand pile to make roads, firm foundations and Jurassic Parks.

"Get the hose," ordered Ben.

He was the construction foreman and the artificial lake was ready to be filled. His cousin Matt participated in the project.

"This island is for the raptors," said Matt. Ben had a healthy fear of raptors.

"Pow, pow," said Ben, shooting at the island's creatures. Going into the house, Ben looked under couches and beds and in boxes.

"What's in there?" asked Nanny.

"Raptors."

Ben didn't take his job as raptor hunter lightly.

"Let's go back yonder," said Ben, "and get the raptors."

Yonder was Ben's reference to the bedroom at the far end of the hall at Nanny's house. That was where the crib, stuffed animals, toys, pictures and map-covered walls, and raptors stayed. He walked bravely, flashlight in hand down the hallway. After a few minutes he ran out giggling.

"Raptors, run for it," Ben squealed.

During the hot summer days, Ben looked forward to swimming with his cousins. Ben wore a yellow swim sweater that looked like a tank top T-shirt attached to an inner tube. He had great freedom in it and could paddle his legs to move comfortably around the pool while his cousins fought off shark attacks.

"This is the life," Lyndy once said, while floating on her back during a quiet lull. "It just doesn't get any better."

And when you thought about it, breathing in deeply and letting all the tension out, she was right.

Now summer had faded, and the pool was closed. We

loaded into the cars to drive to the property, as we called Lyndy's house, to visit and eat supper. There was food to accommodate all tastes: fried rice, hot dogs, and pizza.

After supper, the kids retreated upstairs for play.

"Presenting the world's greatest superheroes," Matt announced to the grown-ups still talking in the kitchen.

Out walked Ben and Lyndy dressed as Batman and Superman. Lyndy pushed back the hood of the Batman costume which was oversized and kept falling over her eyes. Then just as quickly as they had appeared they ran off and up the stairs.

After a brief change, they were back with Matt calling for attention.

"Don't be afraid of the wild creatures you're about to see, we think we have the situation under control."

Holding hands, a dragon and tiger crept into view. Katie, wearing a safari hat, and holding a doll chair in one hand, and a ribbon which she used as a make-believe whip in the other, held the creatures at bay.

Again they quickly disappeared.

"For your enjoyment, the world's greatest fashions," said Matt, bowing.

Katie, Lyndy and Ben were dressed in huge shirts, boas around their necks and feathery hats. Hints of make-up smudged their faces.

The appreciative audience 'ooh-ed' and 'ah-ed'.

Finally, Matt returned.

"The last guest of the day is from the ballet."

Ben tip-toed in with pink tights, tutu and tiara. They all clapped and laughed. Papa made a photo which Ben would place later on his refrigerator door at home with magnets.

"Bath time," Aunt Cathy announced as the kids went scurrying up the stairs.

I gathered our belongings for the trip home. Nanny and Papa packed up food for Ben and me to take along.

Upstairs, the kids argued about who could take a bath with Ben.

The sun was setting when Papa carried Ben to the car for the departure. Ben gave kisses by pressing his cheek next to each one. His head rested on the pillow as he rode quietly with me along the country lane while the shadows stretched longer and darker across the fields.

"Is it still morning time?" Ben asked.

"Not right now," I answered softly, "It's evening time...the sun's going down, and then it will be nighttime."

"Why's it not morning time?"

"Because the sun's going down and the moon's coming up."

Into the darkening night we drove. Streaks of headlights and red dots of taillights occasionally painted the highway. Our car hummed as we cut through the wind and passed over the roadway, and somewhere between here and there, Ben leaned his head on his pillow and quietly closed his eyes.

***

HALLOWEEN

***

"Maybe I could be a cowboy," announced Ben. "I could wear my cowboy shirt and cowboy hat."

For weeks leading up to Halloween, Ben had been planning his costume. His cowboy hat was a tan Australian outback style hat. It had a wide brim which was the key feature of a cowboy hat. His cowboy shirt was a checkered flannel shirt. He would wear jeans and a red bandana to complete the outfit.

"I need some boots, Tim," said Ben. That's what he had begun to call me, instead of Dad.

Cowboys had to be properly outfitted. I suggested checking with Ben's cousin for boots.

"I could carry my gun here in my pocket," said Ben.

I felt a twinge of concern. I didn't want to encourage guns, but I didn't want to draw undue attention to something so obviously part of being a cowboy. After all, it was a costume and Ben was simply making it complete according to the television depictions. I was glad that Ben hadn't adopted the traits of the popular chop 'em up martial arts cartoon characters. It seemed to me that all kids used some sort of aggressive behavior to empower themselves and confront their fears. A child has to feel capable of self-protection, after all. The key was to help the child focus this need in a healthy way, I thought. The world could be a scary place.

Ben's cousin didn't have any cowboy boots but instead offered snow boots, which fit the feet and temperament. For a while, Ben was satisfied to answer the question, "What are you gonna be for Halloween?" with the sure response, " I'm gonna be a cowboy." In the grocery stores, displays showed haunted houses covered with cobwebs, ghosts, witches and ghouls - but no cowboys.

Ben heard more details: trick or treat, walking to neighbors' houses after dark, and candy. A few days before Halloween it rained. I recalled earlier years when it seemed always to rain on Halloween. Ben didn't have a raincoat and agreed it was time to go shopping. From a store at the mall, we found a shiny yellow coat with buckles. Ben liked to wear it in the light rain.

When Halloween arrived, rain was in the forecast. Around four o'clock, Ben said he didn't want to go trick or treating. It wasn't raining but an active day and the impending darkness dampened his enthusiasm. Around five o'clock, the sun was going down. The doorbell rang and Ben raced to look through the sidepanel curtains. It was his friend from down the street with parents in tow. I opened the door and let them in to grab treats.As they were readying to depart, Ben asked if he could go along.

"What are you gonna be?" I asked.

"I'm gonna be a fireman," and Ben got his raincoat and boots from the closet. I got a flashlight and we walked into the night following the spotlight and friends.

SECRETS

***

"It's a secret," said Ben.

Something new here, I thought. Ben was sitting on the kitchen counter helping me fix supper. Ben had just pushed the toaster lever down as he had seen me do many times before.

"What's the secret," I asked.

Ben didn't want to tell. He smiled.

"You don't tell secrets," said Ben.

"You don't have to keep secrets from me," I said.

"Yes, it's a secret," he affirmed.

I saw that if I pushed too hard Ben might cry.

"Who do you have secrets with?"

"With Matt, and Katie, and you," Ben smiled again.

"And anybody else," I asked trying one more approach.

"At school," he said.

"Well, if you don't tell me, that's okay, but you shouldn't keep secrets from Mom."

Later, I told Janet about the conversation.

"I'll see if I can find out anything more. Don't push it - it may be his imagination or it may be real. I'll find out," she said. I felt better, though still concerned about the school comment. Janet was somehow better at encouraging open conversations with Ben, so I knew she'd get to the bottom of this.

That night, during bathtime, Janet talked to Ben.

"I pushed somebody and I had to sit alone at lunchtime," he revealed.

"You know you shouldn't push anybody," Janet said. "It's not nice and it could hurt somebody."

"Okay, I won't," Ben promised.

After Ben had gone to bed, Janet and I talked about the explanation. I wondered if Ben might have made it up.

"Probably not," she said. "That's a pretty detailed explanation. But you should ask his teacher."

"Should I call her now?" I worried.

"I wouldn't bother her now. Just ask her if anything happened at school when you take him next time."

During our next visit to Clarksville, I discussed Ben's 'secret' with Nanny and Cathy. They appreciated the concern that I felt and agreed with Janet's suggestion.

"Of course, don't encourage him to keep secrets from you either," said Cathy. She commented on my words that it was okay to keep secrets from me but not his mom. I realized the truth here, too.

"Did anything happen at school last Friday? I mean, did Ben push anybody? He said he did and had to sit alone at lunch," I asked his teacher the next school day, speaking softly and away from the kids.

"Yes, he did," Ben's teacher said, with a reassuring look.

Ben was not making it up. She explained Ben seemed

a little out of sorts, and while in lunch line pushed another child beside him. She told him not to, but he seemed to be challenging her directions.

"Well, you handled it fine," I said. "If it happens again please let me know so I can work with him at home. I don't want him hitting others."

"Oh, he didn't hit. It was more like nudging. I think it was more in response to my authority than anything," she said. "Don't worry it's a phase they all go through. I've had to do this with others - several others!"

***

THANKSGIVING

***

"I wanted to be an Indian," Ben said.

"Pilgrims are okay, maybe next year you can be an Indian," I said.

We were talking about Ben's preschool program in our kitchen. It was about seven in the morning. I drank my morning coffee, Ben his hot chocolate. The rest of the house was quiet.

Janet's mother, whom we called Mammie, and Janet's sister Joyce had arrived Tuesday night and planned to stay through Sunday. Joyce was the chef and directed the purchases of dressing and gravy ingredients necessary for the approaching Thanksgiving feast. Mammie purchased the turkey at a turkey farm before leaving her home near Cincinnati. A tradition started no doubt by her parents, the Frischolz.

"I liked the friendship soup," I said.

At Ben's preschool at the Forest Hills Baptist Church, all the parents and children were invited to contribute to the making of the soup for the families to share on the last day before the Thanksgiving break. I enjoyed meeting the other parents, most of whom I had seen previously but hadn't gotten to know well. The children all knew I was Ben's dad because I picked Ben up before rest time each day.

"Ben, your dad's here," one of the children would announce.

I volunteered to help the children learn the computer for an hour a week, and got to meet each one individually. I was amazed at the varied personalities.

One time a preschooler asked me what I did. I said I raised Ben full-time at home.

"I mean what do you do, what kind of work?" he asked again.

I understood the context better and told him I was a lawyer. Now he seemed satistifed.

"I wish my dad was a lawyer, so he could stay home with me," he said.

Nanny's side of the family had gathered for Thanksgiving since the beginning of my memory. Looking at pictures of the earlier meetings, we played a game of guessing the year and place. The dinner rotated annually. This year was our first as hosts.

The night before, we cleared out the great room and set up tables and chairs, enough to seat forty. The dinning room seated eight and was the place of honor for Nanny and her sisters. The kitchen seated four, and the counters held the pot luck of vegetables and desserts.

"Are we gonna have friendship soup, today?" Ben asked early on Thanksgiving Day.

"Today, Joyce is cooking. You'll have to ask her," I said.

"Alright," he said.

It was still early so Ben and I went to the room over the garage. I turned on the television to check the Weather Channel. Cloudy, high in the 50s, and a cool drizzle likely. I punched the remote until something caught my eye. PBS was showing seven straight hours of *A Year In Provence* - what a gustatory coincidence.

In *Provence* they would roast chicken on a spit while we would roast succulent turkey, well-basted, for hours. They would saute truffles while we baked oyster stuffing. They would drink wine and we would drink tea, milk, and coffee. They ate baguettes and Camembert while we feasted on hot buttered yeast rolls and sorghum molasses. On and on went the mouth-watering feasts.

"I can't wait any longer," Ben said. "Let's wake Joyce up and start cooking."

***

CONNECTIONS

***

"Do you want to glue some?" I asked.

Ben liked using Elmer's glue. He had a large bottle. Large enough to caulk the whole bathroom, I imagined. In fact, the company should have made a caulk gun dispenser for glue and Ben would have been its chief proponent because of the perfect combination of two of Ben's favorite subjects: arts and crafts, and real tools. I puzzled over the inventions that popped into my head. These connections were borrowed, I knew, from the viewpoint of a three-year-old.

"Get the glue," said Ben, trying to stir me from daydreaming.

I got the glue, construction paper, and scissors. Ben used the scissors while I held the paper rigid. Cutting paper required teamwork because the scissors were plastic, for safety, and unable to cut like metal scissors. I wondered if the manufacturer realized its product fostered collaboration. Once some pieces had been lopped off, gluing began with intensity.

"Not too much in one spot," I advised.

Ben liked to watch the string of glue form puddles. He set the bottle down and picked a triangle shape of cut paper. As the white cream oozed beyond the dimensions of the piece, Ben smeared the paper around like a mop.

Snip, squeeze, press. This work continued unabated until the pile of clippings disappeared.

"Looks pretty good," said Ben arising and walking to the bathroom. "I need to wash my hands."

He pulled his stepstool near the sink and held his arms out over the basin.

"Can you roll up my sleeves?" he asked.

Ben enjoyed the running water for a moment and then turned to me abruptly.

"I need to go pee-pee," he announced.

I turned off the faucet and dried his hands. Ben had mastered this part of potty training last August, I recalled, as a wave of satisfaction and relief washed over me. Ben finished and flushed the commode.

"Why is it so loud?" he asked.

"That's the sound of the water," I said.

"I wish it wasn't so loud," Ben said.

"Maybe you can invent a quiet flush," I smiled. And I thought of the benefits of such a device.

"I have to wash my hands," Ben said as he stepped back up on his stool. Ben squeezed some soap from a sponge into the sink.

"I'm cleaning, I like to clean."

Often Ben would clean, dustbust, windex, or mop because he enjoyed the activity as a form of play.

Ben directed me in completing chores.

"I'm having a hard time," said Ben when frustration or fatigue occurred. And after scrubbing and mopping for a while this is what Ben always said.

"Let's have a snack," I suggested.

"Good idea. And some water," he agreed.

"I think we've done enough cleaning for right now."

"But we have to do more."

"There'll always be more. Let's have an outing," I said.

"But I want to stay here," he declared.

"How about a walk up to the mountain hut?"

Ben liked this idea so we bundled up in our coats, hats, and gloves and set out the backdoor.

The mountain hut was an eight by eight playhouse made of plywood that stood at the top of the hill on our property. It was obscured by the dense forest but accessible by a deerpath.

Ben trudged up the hill like a little Trojan. Head down, hands positioned to catch himself if he slipped. I followed with hands on knees for a boost. We reached the hut, unlatched the door, and entered to survey the damage by woodland critters. Squirrels had long ago discovered and made the hut a shelter from the storms. Edges of wood showed the lighter tan from gnawing.

"Looks pretty good," said Ben and set off up the mountain.

Ben found paths where none existed to me, forcing me to crouch under tree limbs and block with my forearms the abrasive branches and twigs.

"Here's a good path," said Ben, striking off again

through another impenetrable thicket.

"No, it's not very good for me. How about over here," I suggested.

Sometimes Ben would change course and sometimes not. I sweated as I walked twice the distance, having to zig-zag across the paths chosen by Ben. Size was a definite advantage. Being smaller and closer to the earth, Ben could see almost limitless opportunities that weren't available to me.

There was a rustle under the leaves.

"What's that?" asked Ben. Stone-still, we surveyed the forest floor.

"Maybe a squirrel," I said.

"Maybe a rabbit," said Ben.

"Or a mouse."

All quiet, we slowly moved onward and upward.

"Let's pause for a second," I suggested as we came to a clearing.

I breathed deeply and felt my muscles relax as tension rose off me. The wind blew gently, cooling the beads of water on my temples. Virtual reality would never duplicate this, I imagined, and my endorphins agreed.

"This is a good path," said Ben and he was away in a flash.

Nearing the top, we hiked lightly, upright. The underbrush thinned out and outcroppings of limestone appeared.

"Let's sit here," said Ben.

The leafless trees afforded a clear view of the valley which stretched out below us and on to the river. Some bottomland had been plowed under, some still covered and yet untouched. No implements rusting in the fields that I could see.

"Is this north?" asked Ben.

"It is," I said. "And down through there is south where our house sits."

"And what's that?" he asked.

"What do you mean?"

"Is that west?"

"Yes, it is," I said.

"Why is that west?" he wondered.

We had talked before about the earth as a ball turning round and round as it moved around the sun.

"The sun goes down in the west in the nighttime, and in the morningtime it comes up over there in the east," I explained.

"Why is it not morningtime?" asked Ben.

"Because it's almost nighttime. The sun's going down."

Ben picked up a stick and moved leaves around on the ground by his foot. For a minute he watched a worm wriggling.

"You don't smush it, it's a good worm," he said as I listened intently, "It's okay to touch it."

But he didn't touch it, he just watched and pushed the leaves away to give it more space.

"Worms are small to live underground," he explained. "You don't want to touch snakes."

"Do you not like snakes?" I asked.

Ben said, "I don't like snakes. And I don't like alligators, just ordinary people."

And then he looked toward the west.

"Is it morningtime in China?" he asked.

"It will be," I said. "When it's nighttime here, it's morningtime in China."

We had talked about this before and Ben no doubt would talk about it again.

"Is it far, far away?" he asked.

"Yes, it is. We would have to fly in an airplane, and it would take a long time."

"Why is it so far away?" asked Ben. "I wish it was closer."

The sky blinked and blushed. Ben and I stood and stretched, and deeply inhaled the night scent. Then quietly, softly we stepped through the shadows of twilight down the mountain toward home.

***

WINTER

Even a child is known by his doings,
whether his work be pure,
and whether it be right.

-Proverbs 20:11

THE WISE MAN
***

"Is it gonna be a free day?" asked Ben.

He meant: do I go to school today? Ever since the police had visited the preschool class and talked about strangers, Ben had reservations about happily going to school. His teachers said that the police officer may have talked a bit above their level, because by the end of the talk, each teacher was craddling two or three kids in her lap.

"Yes, today is a free day," I said. "But it's also the day of your Christmas program." For weeks, the class had made decorations and planned the performance.

"We wish you were Mary Christmas, and a Happy New Year," sang Ben.

Interesting version, I thought, and it works fine. Ben and I played the chords on the guitar and sang together.

"Why isn't it 'twinkle, twinkle, little star'?" asked Ben.

The words had been changed but the tune was indeed that of the old childhood classic.

Songs were changed for different reasons, I explained to Ben. These words fit Christmas, I offered.

As I thought about it I realized that the ending of the 'ABC' song was also different now from the version I had grown up with. No longer was it "...Now I've said my

ABCs, tell me what you think of me." Now children sang, "...Now I've sung my ABCs, next time won't you sing with me." Things change with the times.

Ben adjusted to the new words fine. There were six lines and Ben had memorized all of them.

"Today, I'll come with you to the school program," I said.

"And you won't leave me today ever again, at all, not once," he said.

"Right."

We loaded into the car and drove down the road singing and humming. The parking lot was full of cars. In Ben's classroom, kids were in various states of undress. There were angels, and shepherds, and wisemen.

"This is your costume," said one of the helpers handing a hanger to Ben.

I took the hanger and began to dress Ben in the floor-length robe, tie, and felt vest. Then Ben got to try on a crown. Finally, he was given a bottle to carry.

"This is a gift for the baby," said Ben.

Ben started to mingle with the others and I backed off to videotape the scene.

The three-year-old class was the opening act. They entered from stage right. They seemed seasoned, not at all nervous, in front of the crowd of parents and under the glare of at least a dozen, maybe twenty, video cameras.

Once on stage, by the pulpit, Ben walked to the microphone and pulled it a little lower. He stepped back in line. The teacher began the singing.

"Twinkle, twinkle, special star..." and "...We wish you were Mary Christmas."

Ben swayed his head as he sang. He cradled the bottle in his hands, careful not to drop the baby's gift.

When finished, they all took seats on the front row and watched the other classes perform.

One group sang Hallelujah, over and over and over, which rolled out stronger and shorter each time until it sounded like a sneeze. Someone standing behind me quietly said, "Gesundheit."

As the performances clipped by, one boy waved and called to his mom. That drew warm laughter from the audience. Another boy fled from the stage having burst into tears upon realizing that a house of grown-ups confronted him. That brought a collective 'aw' of heartfelt sympathy from the audience as the boy embraced his mom.

Afterwards, cookies and punch were served in the reception room.

"You did just fine, Ben. Did you have fun?" I asked.

"I did," he affirmed.

"That was a very nice Christmas program, and I have it on video," I said. The video was still rolling, "Is there anything you want to tell everybody about Christmas?"

Ben straightened his crown.

"Sometimes you have to adjust the microphone."

And that was all he would say.

***

I wondered if Ben understood any of the magic of Christmas. I observed as Ben and Janet made lists for Santa, and looked through catalogs that seemed to spontaneously regenerate inside the mailbox during this season.

"What's your name?" Janet would ask, and then, "How old are you?"

Ben liked this game.

She asked, "Have you been a good boy?" and then, "What do you want Santa to bring you?"

Ben practiced the right answers: "Ben, three, I have; and a smoking grill, a train, a fire engine."

Ben helped Janet decorate the tree.

"I wish we had lights to put outside the house," he said.

We didn't have lights for outside so one night we drove around looking at the neighborhood light displays.

Janet took Ben to a friend's house to make and decorate Christmas cookies. Ben was a natural baker. Could this be the perfect season for a three-year-old, I wondered.

Christmas eve was spent at Nanny and Papa's for a family dinner and present opening.

"Here's another one...open it...more..," Ben's eyes glistened as he danced from tree to present.

"Who gave that boy some nog?" said a voice behind the shower of flying paper.

Christmas Day itself was more quietly observed alone at home. Ben played with his new toys for hours. Nothing wrong with his concentration. Turkey roasting in the oven. Mouth-watering. Soothing blasts of heat and aroma from the opened oven door.

I set the table while Ben and Janet played in the den which was situated up the steps from the kitchen above the garage. Ben called it the workshop. I listened to the muffled voices from the workshop and smiled as if a shroud covering the true magic of the season had momentarily been lifted.

"Do you like your presents?" asked Janet.

"I do," said Ben and he stood very still looking around his workshop. A look of concern crossed his face. And Ben quietly, softly spoke so only Janet could hear.

"I got so many things, I hope Santa has enough for all the other boys and girls."

***

IN THE SPRINGTIME
***

A heavy January frost lay on the ground, and for that matter on the bushes and rooftops. I liked to clean out files on days like these. Old papers that had been saved for some forgotten reason were piled up now to be discarded.

Ben helped by drawing on the papers strewn about the living room floor.

"Get some scissors and glue and tape," said Ben.

Projects that were once cut and dried assumed a literal meaning. I held a piece of typing paper while Ben manipulated the scissors. We were both getting better at collaboration. Some papers would be ripped either by accident or on purpose. Then a glop of Elmer's would find itself to some part of the disarray to which another shred of paper would be pressed. The collage was art: After all, I had seen bits of paper randomly stuck to boards, framed and hung on the walls of prestigious businesses. Just a day ago, I noticed such a piece at McDonald's. The theme was recycling.

I liked to try to duplicate Ben's work, but never seemed to get the same effect. My pieces were soft and lifeless compared to the vibrancy of Ben's. Even the stray pen marks, though not depictions of things recognizable to me, were impossible to duplicate. Random marks were not just random marks anymore. I recalled a remark I attributed to Picasso: It takes a long time to become young. It somehow made sense as I now watched Ben.

"I'll put these away," I said.

"But I need 'em," he said.

I made a pile of discards which we would use for cutting and pasting. The rest I crammed back into the file drawer.

"What about those?" asked Ben, obviously interested in the papers being put out of reach.

"We'll go through those later," I said. "In the springtime."

Ben turned his attention back to the pile of papers on the floor. For the rest of the morning, we cut and tore, and some we crumpled. Then we glued and pressed the collage together. Ben made some lines and dots with a pen. Finally, Ben made me write "Do not throw away" on the finished piece.

Later, after lunch, we played in the garage. It was warmer than the winter day outside but still cool. Too cool to just sit and paint. Or stand and even hammer or saw, though we tried this for a while. Ben decided he needed to make a web. I got a ball of string out of the tool closet and handed it to Ben who began immediately to unwrap it.

I stepped outside to survey the grounds. I wanted to load up the dismantled wooden airplane that Papa had made for Ben and carry it to the dumpster. The airplane had seen dozens of imaginary flights, but heavy use and weathering had weakened the wood in spite of our efforts of painting and regular maintenance.

Meanwhile, Ben wrapped the string around the doorknob. He looked around the room. With string in hand, he unwound it and walked to the far wall. There he wrapped it around his wagon, then back to the middle and right for a few wraps around the support pole. Back and forth he moved.

I decided that this would be a good day for a visit to the dumpster. I opened the hatch to the car which I had moved outside to make room in the garage for Ben to play. I backed my car close to the plane. Slowly, I positioned the fuselage next to the rear hatch. It wouldn't fit fully into the car. I would need to tie the hatch down for the transport. I could use Ben's twine.

When I tried to open the backdoor leading to the garage, it wouldn't budge.

"No trespassing," said Ben.

"No trespassing?" I said to myself. I pressed my face to the window, cupping my hands around my face to block the glare.

"What the..." and my voice trailed off as I laughed at my predicament. I saw that Ben had tied the twine around most every object in the garage.

"Ben, can you open the door and let me in?"

"In just a minute," came the reply.

It was cold outside in the shade of the house where the backdoor was located.

"I'd really like to come in now," I said.

Ben walked over to the door and turned the knob. He grinned. It wouldn't budge.

"Can you open it?" asked Ben.

I looked around as Ben walked back to spinning his web.

"Ben, please try again."

"Why?"

I thought. The cold wasn't much motivation, Ben was fine in the garage.

"I need you to come with me to the dumpster," I said.

Ben had liked to take things to the dumpster before, surely this would motivate him.

Ben came over to the door again.

"Why do we need to come to the dumpster?"

"I want to load the airplane in the car. It would be a good day to go."

"No it wouldn't." And Ben stood there looking through the panes.

"Just a second," said Ben as he turned and stepped back. His little hand reached up and pressed the automatic garage door opener. I remembered then that I also had an door opener in my car.

"Thanks," I said as I quickly entered the garage. Quite a web you've made here." Ben thought so too.

"You want to help me take the plane to the dumpster?" I said half-heartedly.

It was a big project, and I was recalling the cold which

Ben had rescued me from.

"Not right now," said Ben.

"Well, we ought to do it sometime, that old plane is falling apart."

Ben looked at Papa's plane in which he had had so much fun.

"Let's take it..." and he paused in thought again, and finished. "...in the springtime."

And so we did.

***

IT'S YUCKY

***

After several bedtime stories, Ben lay quietly. He was covered, nightlight on, and door pulled to. Janet and I settled down and reminded each other of times and things to do tomorrow. We watched Jay Leno and listened as he made jokes about the events of the day. Eventually, the tensions of the day faded and fatigue took hold and we went to sleep.

After midnight, Ben started crying.

"I'll go this time," I said. Janet usually attended to night callings. After years as a doctor, she functioned better in the wee hours. This time, though, she agreed and rolled back over to sleep.

I sat on the floor beside Ben's bed and rubbed his back. Ben sobbed lightly.

"What's wrong, honey?" I asked.

Ben didn't answer at first.

"I was having a bad dream," he said at last.

I continued to rub, and tried to hum something deep and soft. My mind was muddled and I mixed several tunes together.

Ben sat up.

"Wipe my eyes," he said. "I need a drink of water."

I got the water and returned. Ben took a small sip.

"Here, blow," I said holding a tissue to Ben's nose.

"Now lie down and I'll tell you a story."

Ben did as directed and became quieter. After a while, I left.

"He was having a bad dream," I reported to Janet as I returned to bed and covered up.

Sleep didn't return so I lay awake with lids shut to soothe my eyes. Sometimes I would lie awake for hours after having to get up in the middle of a sound sleep, but not tonight. I heard Ben again and slipped quickly and quietly back to Ben's room before the cries became too loud and insistent.

I sat down on the floor again and tried to comfort Ben. Something seemed different this time.

"What's wrong?" I asked. "Another bad dream?"

Ben sat up and leaned on my shoulder. I picked him up and carried him to the spare bedroom where we could both comfortably lie down. Ben pressed his head to my chest. I put my arms around him. The warmth soothed us both. Ben cried softly.

"Are you okay?" asked Janet. She stood next to the bed.

"I think so," I mumbled sleepily.

She reached over to feel Ben, left for a few seconds and returned with a bottle and dropper.

"He feels warm," she said and managed to get Ben to take a dropper of pediatric Tylenol, followed by a sip of water. "You go back to bed, I'll stay up with him a while."

I agreed, this time falling asleep quickly. Sometime later, she crawled back in bed having succeeded in lulling Ben to sleep.

I awoke about six. As I put on coffee, I heard little feet.

"Wipe my eyes," he pleaded as he entered the kitchen.

I picked him up and carried him to the family room. I held him close and stroked his hair.

"Does your head hurt?" I asked.

Ben was holding his hand next to his left jaw. I gently pressed the fleshy underside of my arm over Ben's left ear and jaw and rocked him and hummed. Ben continued to cry softly. I carried him to the kitchen and fixed a cup of half coffee and half milk.

"Try a sip, it's warm not hot," I said.

Ben sipped a little and burrowed closer to me. "Maybe we could see Dr. Mary and get some medicine," he said. I agreed.

It was close to seven and Janet was stirring. I carried Ben to the bedroom.

"Have you been up long?" she asked.

I explained what was up.

"I'll call as soon as their office opens and we'll take him in before they start to see their scheduled patients," she said.

Ben and I drove in together. Janet followed in her car so that after the doctor's visit she could go on to work. Ben rested his head on a pillow as the buzz of the road and heater lulled him to sleep. I was glad to hear the quiet for it meant that the pain had temporarily subsided.

As the car rolled over the asphalt ribbon, I recalled times of pain. Physical pain passed quick enough not to leave many scars. There was the dull ache of my joints, the acute episode of the bulging cervical disc, the torn anterior cruciate ligament in the left knee, and long ago, now only the memory of a memory, the earaches of childhood.

I recalled the memory of painful memories. I saw the little boy that I once was crying. I felt the tightening in my head that had no relief. I felt the wetness of my eyes spill down my cheeks. I felt the heat of the hot water bottle that I clung to like an appendage. I was glad Ben was sleeping. Soon my little son would have some medicine.

At the doctor's office, there were no patients waiting. It was too early to begin but they let Ben, Janet and me back into an exam room. Ben didn't object to the stethoscope, he had practiced with his own at home. And though the other tools were unfamiliar, Ben didn't object. He wanted help, and knew this was the way to get it.

The doctor prescribed drops to numb the ear, pediatric Motrin for the fever, and antibiotics to fight the infection. It ended in a matter of minutes. Ben and I were on our way back home, and Janet on her way to work.

Ben was pretty listless most of the day. Janet called to check on her boys. You could tell that Ben didn't feel well

- he reclined and just watched television. He didn't complain about medicine much either, he knew it would help, or he hoped it would.

"It tastes yucky," was all he would say.

Then he would swallow, chase it with juice.

"But why does it taste yucky?" he asked again.

Even in my slack jaw tired state, I appreciated the question.

***

Nanny had come to stay with us during Ben's convalescence. I lay down for a nap but couldn't sleep. I fixed lunch which Ben nibbled. More medicine. During *Mr. Rogers' Neighborhood*, Ben slept. I recorded it on the VCR. He talked about grandparents. Good timing.

Janet called to encourage me to get sleep in case Ben woke up in the middle of night again. We were both using up valuable reserves. Lounging rejuvenated me even if I didn't sleep.

Sleep. Now there was a topic that deserved attention. No sleep and you're cranky, or running on fumes. Over a long period desperate thoughts are born. Uncle Bro said he had trouble sleeping which he traced back to the year his first child was born. Amused, for some reason, I felt giddy. Light-headed. A good night's sleep seemed precious.

I remembered hearing somewhere that sleep deprivation was the fast lane to insanity. Just close the eyes when you're tired. That should be all it takes to pass out. La la land. I sang la la in my mind. Nothing worked when you tried too hard. The mind was stubborn, like a three-year-old.

I was glad for my mother's help. I squeezed my eyes shut. This made the eyes water soothingly. Isometric exercise for the lids above, and soft tissue forming the deepening circles below. Things could be worse, my muddled mind told me. Ben could be struggling with a brain tumor like his cousin, Nathan. I would have to expend energy in the rush to the emergency room, and endless trips to hospitals. Ben, like Nathan, could be enduring endless chemo and radiation therapies, or surgeries. And there would be so many tears.

None of this had happened, of course, nor would it happen to Ben, but at this moment I wrestled the diaphanous demons halfway between reality and dream, and could not know this.

Eventually, Ben and Janet and I got the healing sleep we needed.

"Not much else matters when you're sick," I said. "It's yucky."

"But why is it yucky?" Ben asked again.

And I knew Ben felt much better, because Ben answered himself.

"It just is," he said.

***

DISTRACTIONS

***

"I didn't want an operation," said Ben as Janet held him in the recovery room.

On Friday the 13th, Ben had surgery to repair a hydrocele, a child's hernia. Nanny and Papa spent the night before and after the surgery at our house. In the recovery room, Ben asked for Nanny. Nanny and Janet held him and rocked him and told him stories to distract him from the discomfort.

"I see two Nannys," said Ben once the pain medication kicked in.

Ben didn't like the IV in his arm. Nor did he like the gown.

"Take this off now," he said as the pain subsided. "I'm ready to put on my jeans. I'm ready to go now."

About two hours had passed since the surgery and our entourage departed heading for home. Much of the afternoon was spent watching cartoons, napping, eating ice cream, and telling stories. By evening time, Ben felt much better.

"Do you want to play with Play-Doh?" he asked.

Papa and Ben rolled out the Play-Doh and cut pieces for pretend cooking. Ben shuttled back and forth to Nanny giving her samples. From Janet, he required a menu which she wrote out and gave to him.

"This is the menu, Nanny," Ben said. "I'll bring you the food."

He went back to Papa and supervised the preparation. Ben brought out some Doh and promptly took it back.

"I'd like to speak to the manager." Nanny said.

"I am the manager," said Ben, not missing a beat.

I was in the kitchen getting supper ready. Ben entered sucking a lozenge in his mouth.

"I have a nutcracker in my mouth," he smiled revealing the lozenge and crunching it with his teeth. I winced.

"Here's the menu," he added.

"Good menu," I said, accepting the menu.

"I'll bring the Play-Doh down here and we can fix biscuits."

"Why don't we make real ones?" I suggested.

"Okay, get the Bisquick," said Ben.

We arranged the box, bowl, spoon and milk on the counter. Ben sat on the counter ready to cook. I poured the ingredients together and Ben stirred.

"Now let's roll the dough in the flour," said Ben. This was his favorite part.

"Keep it powdery, so it doesn't stick to your hands too much," I said. We rolled and cut tiny biscuits and put them on the pan and into the oven.

"Wash up," said Ben. I cleaned his hands and set him on the floor. Ben scrambled away to the others. "We're making biscuits," he announced in the next room.

He crawled onto the couch between Nanny and Janet. They told stories and read picture books while Papa joined me to finish getting supper ready.

"You look tired. Go rest, I'll finish," Papa said.

"I'm okay, just thinking," I said.

"About anything in particular?"

"Not really, just relieved Ben's okay," I said as we both puttered about the kitchen. I left and returned in a minute with a picture which I showed to Papa.

"That's a happy child," Papa said as he looked at the smiling face of the boy surrounded by Mickey Mouse and Goofy.

"His name is Nathan," I said. "Son of Janet's cousin. They took a trip to Disneyworld." I didn't mention anything about Nathan's brain tumor.

"That's where you all should go," Papa said.

"We plan to later when Ben's older."

"Don't wait too long," Papa said. "Before you know it'll be too late."

***

GARDENING

***

"Did you not smash your fingers?" asked Ben as I shut the backdoor behind us.

"No. Are your fingers okay?"

"Sure," he nodded.

Ben found this question important ever since he had shut the door on the tip of his right ring finger. Of course, he didn't wear a ring, but that nevertheless was the finger. He didn't lose the nail either, though it was sore for awhile afterward. I had tried to remain calm and hold an ice pack to it. I had never been especially good with loud noises like crying or yelling, because I tended to lose composure. I was pleased to see improvements in my own composure since caring for my three-year-old son.

"We need to turn the garden for planting when spring arrives," I said. Middle Tennessee was having a February thaw, a regular occurrence during which the temperatures moderate in the mid-60s and a warm southerly breeze blows for several days.

"That'd be a good idea," agreed Ben. From the tool closet in the garage, we got a hoe, pickax, and rake.

"Don't forget the hand protection," said Ben.

"Okay." I got the gloves. "Your glove is a little jabberwockyed." But together we managed to slip and pull on the glove.

"That's it," Ben said, and then the next glove fit in place.

"Do you want to wear the hard hat?" I asked.

"That's alright. You can wear it," Ben answered.

I chopped the soil and Ben scraped it to the edge. We alternated the tools frequently. After scraping the soil, we pushed it back over the exposed hard packed ground. Then Ben started raking it smooth while I picked up twiddles. Ben put down his implement.

"Whew, I need something to drink."

I left to fetch a cup of water. Ben drank thirstily.

"You finish it," he said.

While I drank, Ben went around the corner to the garage and returned with the red Radio Flyer wagon.

"Help," he summoned.

"What's wrong?" I asked.

"I can't get it up these steps," said Ben.

I lumbered slowly over and lifted the wagon off the driveway to the back walk. Ben pulled the wagon further, positioning it next to the dig site. He began to pick up the twiddles, while I, feeling the drain of exertion during the lull of gardening work, stretched.

"Help me pull it," said Ben, referring to the wagon load. We rolled the wagon to the hillside where the woods began, dumped the twiddles, and returned the wagon to its resting place in the garage.

"I need my eye protection," Ben said.

"What for?" I asked as I retrieved the goggles from

the tool closet.

"I want to weed-eat."

I got the Toro weedeater down off its hook. We held it together and walked outside. With gloves and goggles in place, he pulled the safety and trigger with one hand and held the whipping cord to the grass. We clear cut circles of grass that reminded me of the geometric patterns cut in the croplands of England by unrevealed forces.

"Have you ever been to England?" I asked, but the motor was too loud for Ben to hear.

After a while, Ben released the trigger and we stopped.

"I need to pee," he said.

"Let's put this away and..."

"No, I need to pee now."

And Ben trotted around the corner to the garden. As I rounded the corner, Ben had his britches around his knees and was letting loose with a high arcing stream.

"I had to empty my bladder," said Ben, using the phrase he learned after his operation.

"Yeah, me too," I said.

***

THIRTY-ONE AND A HALF
(IT'S THE THOUGHT THAT COUNTS)
***

"I wish somebody was sitting in that other chair," said Ben.

Ben, Janet and I were seated at the breakfast table which was circular and had four chairs. Mostly we ate on TV trays or standing and moving or in shifts to accommodate Ben's active nature and interest. But this meal was a rare sit-down affair only in the sense that we all were sitting and eating at the same time and place.

"Who would you like to sit there?" asked Janet.

"Somebody like another Ben," he said without a moment's hesitation.

Judging by the smile on his face and glint in his eyes you could tell that he liked himself and other kids. His cousins had visited over the past weekend. Matt, Katie and Lyndy could be a rowdy bunch. And Ben fit in well.

Together they had enough energy to power the TVA. Or so it seemed to me. Ben loved to spin around dizzily, figuratively and literally, when they were together. Ben would pretend he was the world turning round and round as I had explained to him and holler, "Night and day," over and over.

"Another Ben would be nice," said Janet. "Because we think you're fabulous."

"Next weekend is Matt's birthday party," I said. "And we'll see all the kiddles again. That'll be fun."

"That will be fun," echoed Ben.

Janet and I had thought about more kids but considered ourselves mighty lucky in middle age to have Ben.

Later that day, Ben asked more questions about Matt's birthday. Ben liked to light candles and sing and blow them out. A fleeting ceremony, I thought, how appropriate to mark the passage of time.

"Can we make a cake for Matt?" asked Ben.

"Sure," I said, though I didn't quite know how since I didn't have a mix on hand. "But we have to go to the store and get a cake mix."

"But we have ingredients," said Ben.

He walked around the counter and pulled his stool closer. Climbing up, it was obvious he planned to scale the countertop and rummage in the cupboards. I stood nearby to steady him.

Ben opened the cupboard door.

"See we have flour up there." Of course, he was right. I kept a few staples like flour and baking powder stocked for biscuits.

"Okay, I guess we can do it," I said, not fully convincing myself.

We arranged the ingredients on the counter: flour, sugar, milk, egg, vanilla, salt, electric mixer, measuring cup, spoon, and mixing bowl. Somewhere in the recesses of my mind lingered a recipe passed down from my grandmother: thirty-one and a half. That would be a good start, I thought.

"First we add three cups of flour. Then one cup of sugar. Then one-half cup of milk." I spoke aloud to convince myself.

"Can I mix it now?" said Ben reaching for the electric mixer.

"Not yet, let me stir a little with the spoon," I said. "Hmm, not enough milk." I poured more milk until the ingredients were the consistency of pudding.

"Now I can mix," said Ben. We held the buzzing machine together to keep splattering to a minimum.

"Want to taste?" I asked. Ben had tried my concoctions before and now declined, so I tasted the whipped batter.

"Too floury." I pronounced the mixture. I added drops of vanilla and a few shakes of salt. "Still not right."

"Let's add an egg," suggested Ben and before I could move the whole egg lay in the bowl.

"We have to crack it first, Ben," I explained. I picked out the slightly cracked egg and most of the shell, then split it and let the yolk drop in the bowl.

Ben held the mixer ready and then dropped it in the bowl. There wasn't too much batter on it so we didn't wipe it before turning on the power.

"It looks like gak," said Ben.

Some of the batter found its way across the vastness of space and landed on my eyebrow. I smeared the 'gak' across my forehead in an attempt to wipe it clean.

"Want to taste now?" I asked.

"You try it," Ben said warily.

I stuck my finger in the bowl and licked it.

"Almost perfect. Let's add cinnamon," I said.

The phone rang. It was Nanny. I talked as I stirred the mixture with a spoon.

"What recipe did you use?" asked Nanny.

"No recipe, it's from scratch," I said proudly. I explained that I recalled a formula of Granny Holladay's that she had used in the past.

"Remember thirty-one and a half," I said and described the addition of other ingredients.She laughed lightly, only just barely audible over the phone.

"That's the recipe for pie crust," she said. "Three cups of flour, one of lard and a half cup of water."

"Oops," I grinned.

"It's the thought that counts," she reminded before hanging up.

"We need to bake it at 350 for 30 minutes," said Ben.

That sounded about right to me, after all that's what I always said when we baked pork chops. We poured the batter into a loaf pan, turned on the oven and timer to the prescribed settings.

"When it's finished we can add icing," I said.

"And candles," said Ben. "But we can't eat it."

No kidding, I thought.

"We'll save it for Matt," Ben said.

MAKING SENSE

***

"Why does he cry so much?" I asked.

Jake continued crying. He was Ben's younger cousin, four months old. His mother, my youngest sister Bess, had left for work and Ben and I were babysitting until Jake's dad Randy got off work and could come by for the pick-up.

"Because he's a little baby," said Ben. And, of course, this made sense.

"Let's play with Play-Doh," suggested Ben.

"I have to hold Jake, but you can bring the Play-Doh here and make something," I said.

"But we have to use it at the table," said Ben.

And, of course, this made sense, too. It was the house rule, and the cutting implements and rollers were at the table.

The crying, strangely, didn't seem quite as bad as when Ben was little. Was I more used to it or was it because this was somebody else's child? Of course, I wasn't thinking very clearly, if at all, with one child wanting to play and another dulling my auditory nerves.

"Let's walk around, let's march," I said. And this Ben did gladly for awhile since it was better than nothing.

"London bridge is falling down..." we sang. Jake stopped crying.

"He likes it," said Ben. This too made sense to me. The little guy was being held, there was activity in the room, and he controlled it all. Interesting, I thought, how everybody reacts to those around them.

After awhile we stopped and Jake remained quiet. I set him down in the bouncy chair. Ben and I talked to him, held stuffed dolls and things up in front of his face and tried to play with him. There was a blue and white soft squeezy doll which was Jake's favorite.

"That's his 'Mouseybear'," observed Ben, who though still attached to his stuffed animal friends was letting go little by little. That made sense, too.

Shortly, Jake was ready for more walking which he signaled by crying again. Walking made him happy. Singing and playing weren't necessary.

"Let's go to the kitchen," said Ben.

"Do you need something?"

"Maybe a snack," said Ben.

On the way the phone rang. It was Randy checking in. Jake must have known for as the receiver was lifted he let out a cry, like he was calling for help - 'come save me from these abductors'- or something like that.

"Is Jake okay?" asked Randy.

"Oh sure," I said. He just won't stop crying, I thought to myself. "I think he wants me to keep walking."

The doorbell rang.

"I'll call if we need anything. We have your number," I said and hung up.

At the door was Ben's aunt Angie, my older sister, who came over to assist for the afternoon. She and Ben would pass the time reading and cutting paper projects while I watched Jake.

"Oh sure," I said. "We were doing fine."

"Jake cries a lot," Ben offered.

"And why does he cry?" she asked.

"I think he's hungry," said Ben.

Since this too made sense, I got the bottle of formula Bess had left in the refrigerator. I heated it slightly in the microwave, and tested it on my wrist. Satisfied it was just right, I offered it to Jake who reached for it as soon as he saw it - supper, at last! I held Jake and the bottle and sat in the recliner. I watched the Weather Channel while Jake closed his eyes and drank. Classical music played on the television while I viewed the current temperatures in Chicago, Denver, St. Louis, and on and on.

You find bliss in the simplest situations.

***

MOM'S FREE DAYS

***

"You take a break, Tim," said Ben.

Janet was home for a week. Instead of traveling to warmer climes, we decided to stay home during her February vacation week. She didn't get to enjoy the homeplace adequately with her busy work schedule, and the amenities were unbeatable not to mention the price. Ben took full advantage of rediscovering his mom, and didn't hesitate to direct me to back off.

"Is tomorrow a free day for you?" Ben asked.

"It sure is, and I have a free day all week," Janet informed him.

"Good." Ben was pleased. They ambled upstairs for a bath.

"Shaving cream crack filler, please," said Ben.

He liked to squirt the cream, pretending it was caulk, in the corners of the tub and fill the cracks. He smoothed it on the walls and shaved the tiles. He had a razor, without the blade, for just such a use. Janet sneezed. The scent of the shaving cream set off her allergies.

"Gesundheit," said Ben. He proudly displayed his skills to Janet. She encouraged him in ways that I didn't.

"When you wash your hair," he said, "you lean back and close your eyes."

Ben rarely washed his own hair when I supervised the

bath, and sometimes I would skip the hair washing. But with Janet, Ben knew, if he didn't wash his hair, she would. Maybe too that's why Ben had more success with 'sit down' potty training with her encouragement. I had helped with the 'stand up' part, however, due in large part with the fun we had peeing in the garden.

"I'm ready to get out now," said Ben.

Out of the bath, dried off, and then to the bed, Ben went for some trampoline action. With Janet on one side and me on the other, Ben began to jump and bounce-walk in circles.

"Two minutes," said Janet.

"Five minutes," countered Ben.

"Stay in the center," I said.

"Stay away from the edge," said Janet.

Ben walked, jumped, climbed off and climbed back on. The rigorous activity played out and he was ready for stories.

"Pick out two books to read," said Janet. Ben examined his books and brought over a pile of about ten books. He spread them out and picked one to start with.

"Robin Hood is good," Ben said, as he and Janet sat back on the pillows to read and look at the pictures.

"That's Little John," he said.

Robin Hood was a fox, and Little John was a bear, and Ben liked them because, among other reasons, they smiled a lot. The villain was a tiger named Prince John.

"He's not mean," said Ben.

"Why is he not mean?" asked Janet.

"Because he's smiling. He doesn't look mean," Ben answered.

Ben found that the sheriff smiled a lot too and announced that he wasn't mean or bad, either.

There were books about trains, farms, construction equipment and imaginary things that didn't have names outside their fantasy on the printed page, and Ben enjoyed them all.

"Time for bed," said Janet.

"I forgot to brush my teeth," said Ben, as he ran to brush them. "But, don't waste water." When he finished, Ben turned to Janet.

"You be Madonna," he said, and he hurried to the chest of drawers and dug out several belts and suspenders.

"Do you even know who Madonna is?" Janet asked.

Ben wrapped several decorative belts around her and then fastened the suspenders over her nightshirt.

"Sure," said Ben.

"I think he remembers that video *Hocus Pocus*. The mother dressed up as Madonna and wore these big cones..." I said.

"Now dance," said Ben.

And we did.

"Well, I think it's about time for bed," I said, finally.

I walked with Ben to his room to tell a bedtime story, but Ben had other plans.

"How about a snack?" he asked.

"No, you've already brushed your teeth," I said as we continued walking.

Then Ben tried another ploy.

"You go take a break, Dad."

"I'll tell him the stories," said Janet, and they continued on into the bedroom.

I seized the opportunity to watch the Weather Channel. After a while, I smelled a delicious buttery aroma and got up to investigate. In the kitchen, I found Ben and Janet feasting on popcorn.

"Looks like I've found Robin Hood and Little John," I said.

"No, silly, it's just me and Mom. She looks like Madonna, that's all." Ben smiled and corrected me.

"What happened to bedtime?" I asked.

"I just don't know. Let me think about it," Ben said, pausing between handfulls. And he did while putting one kernel in his mouth and chewing.

"Mom?" Ben asked.

"Yes, Ben."

"Is it a free day?"

"Yes it is," she replied.

"And Mom?" Ben said.

"Yes, Ben," she smiled.

"Is tomorrow a free day?" he asked.

"It sure is," she said.

Then Ben turned to me. "Tomorrow's a free day. Have some popcorn," he said. And Madonna winked.

IT TAKES A LONG TIME TO BECOME
YOUNG
***

Kids don't make you feel old. They just make you use muscles that haven't been used since you were a kid. Consequently, I ached in places that I hadn't felt for a long time. This made me feel young but tired. Watching Ben go without stop made me realize that our regenerative powers were different. Ben made adjustments as he moved from activity to activity. I stiffened up and stalled like a car that had run out of oil. There must be a way to eliminate the aches without resorting to aspirin but I didn't know what it was.

"I want to ride the caterpillar," said Ben.

He had a peddle-powered plastic tractor, a Caterpeg, with a front loader that fired his imagination. Ben was a construction worker loading leaves or rocks and moving them from one spot to another.

"Whew, this makes me tired," said Ben. He would pause for ten seconds tops and then announce, "I'm all gassed up and ready to go."

Hardly enough time for a coffee break, I thought.

On the road at the end of the street, Ben safely manuevered the Caterpeg round and round faster than I could briskly walk. He must have reached speeds of six or seven miles an hour. To keep me on my toes, Ben turned and sped toward me. At the last second, he veered off.

"I'm coming back for you. Watch out," he laughed.

Ben circled and aimed for me. This time I made the lunge out of the way. Again Ben circled.

"Toro, toro," I yelled.

After the bullfight, Ben peddled up the driveway to the garage.

"Motor assist," said Ben. I pushed him up the grade to the level beside the garage where he parked his Caterpeg.

"How about an outing?" I said.

"But I want to stay here," answered Ben.

Ben easily recognized the ploy. Strapped in the car seats, Ben and I couldn't move, run around and play. There were many more interesting projects possible at home. We could paint, do woodworking, cut and paste paper, read books and work in the garden. It was an idyllic place. It was a grand place to be young.

But then where wasn't, I thought. When you're young, and the world is fresh and new, the fires of the mind and body burn so brightly. At least they should. Briefly the image of Nathan entered my mind. I couldn't help everybody, but I knew I could help at least one child.

Ben called to me and we ran to play.

***

AN OUTING

***

"If we had a camper van, we could sleep in it," said Ben.

"And we could go places and spend the night right in the van," I added.

"Where could we go?" asked Ben.

"Any place we wanted," I said. "We could get a Coleman stove for cooking, and fishing poles too, and live in it when we traveled."

"And we could stand up in it and walk around," said Ben.

"Sure, but not when it was operating," I said.

"Let's do that," said Ben.

I had wanted to do some traveling but wondered if Ben was really up to it. Long trips were hard enough for me let alone a three-year-old. I could hear it now, "Are we there yet?"

Planning a trip wouldn't hurt anything however. And so I did just that.

Uncle Bro had a big VW van that could be outfitted. And Papa had the Coleman stove. Arrangements could be made for a swap for a couple of weeks. Warmer weather would be arriving soon, too. All signs looked positive for an outing. Janet had just finished her vacation though and couldn't get time off again for awhile. We could go it alone, I mused. Famous last words?

On a visit to Clarksville, I kicked the idea around with Papa and Bro.

"You could try the state park and see how it goes," said Papa.

But I was a dreamer and though I agreed, my mind searched for something more exotic.

Back home, I settled down for a little light reading after Ben was quiet in bed. I read my current *Atlantic Monthly* which had arrived that week. My eye settled on a note about the environment: "This month more than half a million sandhill cranes...will descend on an 80-mile stretch of Nebraska's Platte River..."

"Janet," I said. "Ben and I need a little outing. He wants to borrow the camper van and Coleman stove..."

"Where in the world would you go camping?" she asked.

"Oh, it would be on this continent," I assured her.

There's a mystery to the unfolding of events. Tenuous links are made which grow and take on a life of their own. If the path is true you are propelled forward and you hold on for the ride.

***

"Are we there yet? Are we there yet?"

"Wake up," said Janet, as she nudged me from my slumber.

"What? Not yet..." I said as I awoke.

"You've been talking in your sleep," Janet said.

"You've been saying, 'are we there yet' over and over."

"I was dreaming." I rubbed my head, blinked and looked around. "Ben and I were driving to Nebraska to see the cranes, and he kept asking..."

"Are we there yet?" she finished for me.

"Yes, that's what he said," I confirmed.

"You don't have to make this trip," she said.

"But he wants to see the cranes," I said.

We talked a bit, and settled back for sleep again. The cranes flew inside my dreams.

Ben and I were standing on a hill overlooking the Platte River and the vast sprawling landscape. It was quiet in anticipation. A fresh breeze ran its fingers through our hair. Being a dream, we were, of course, naked. On a neighboring hill was a band of angels playing music.

"Digging music," said Ben. The kind of music with a up-tempo, deep bass beat.

Ben was singing 'Wimoweh' and walking in circles. The ground was springy like a trampoline and it cushioned the steps and lifted his feet and knees.

Suddenly, the music stopped as did Ben. All was quiet. Then a low roiling hum swept toward us like thunder, like a rumbling bulldozer, starting far away at the horizon and advancing, unrelenting, on our place on the rise overlooking the river.

We looked to the source and waited. The turbulence continued unabated, increasing in volume and breadth. It was a crashing timpani of jackhammers. Then the skies opened and hurtled its musicians downward. The sandhill cranes speckled the heavens and covered the space about our mound as ants would blacken an anthill. The noise was deafening of wing to wind. Speech was futile for it would not carry to a listener's ear, and so we watched with awe as the migratory procession swooped down to the waters.

***

The next morning, I hummed softly as I made breakfast of bacon and eggs.

"Smells good," said Ben as he walked into the kitchen clutching Mouseybear and his blankey. "That makes me hungry."

I set him on the counter.

"I'll make biscuits," Ben said. I got the Bisquick from the cupboard and we mixed up a batch.

"This is a nice surprise," Janet said as we ate. "What's the occasion?"

"I just felt like it. And I had a pleasant dream about the sandhill cranes," I said.

"I want to see the cranes," said Ben, "Can we find some?"

"Sure," I said.

"See he wants to see them too," I said to Janet.

For now, at least, preparations for the outing would continue.

***

"Is the park far?" asked Ben.

"It's pretty far, but not too much more," I said.

We drove the two lane state route 96 toward Montgomery Bell State Park. This would be a prelude, a warm-up exercise, for the Great Plains trek. We had traveled about 15 miles before Ben asked his first time-place question. But then he was only expecting a trip to the park to see the ducks. (Why is it that kids love ducks?)

We had never been to this park and that reasonably caused some doubt and restlessness. We stopped for directions once and were assured that the park lay not five miles further down the road. Presently, the park entrance sign appeared and Ben was at once relieved and excited. We slowed and rolled down the windows to enjoy the fresh forest air. After a brief circling of sites, we parked near the lake.

"Can we go swimming?" asked Ben.

"It's too cold today but let's walk down to see the water," I said.

We made our way down the steep hillside past the empty picnic tables and grills.

"You should have brought charcoal so we could grill out," said Ben.

"We'll do that sometime when we can bring Mom," I said.

At the bottom we found the swimming area closed.

"What does the sign say?" asked Ben.

"Closed for the season," I said.

"Why is it closed for the season?" asked Ben.

"When the weather gets warmer then it'll be open," I explained.

Beside the swimming area was a boat dock.

"It says closed for the season, too," said Ben. And of course it did.

We walked around and spotted two geese swimming near the pier. We walked out to get a better look.

"Do you have some bread," asked Ben.

"Are you hungry?" I asked.

"Sure," said Ben. "And those ducks might like some, too." I wondered again if all kids loved to feed ducks. The image of Nathan flashed in my mind's eye. I shivered, but not from the weather.

"Well, those are geese, and I don't have any bread for the geese, but if you're hungry we could get lunch at the restaurant over the bridge up that hill," I said and pointed to the lodge.

We ate chicken, potatoes, beans and apples at the lodge. The buffet was all-you-could-eat but our appetites were only big enough for one shared plate. We washed it down with iced tea.

"Can we go see the hotel?" asked Ben pointing out the window toward the wing of the building with rooms.

"Sure," I said.

"One time Nanny and Papa stayed there when the ice storm knocked out the electricity," said Ben.

I was reasonably sure this was not the place they had stayed during last year's ice storm but Ben was right that they had stayed in a motel during the long power outage. In fact, Ben had been at their house when the storm hit.

For two nights they huddled around the gas fireplace which heated the living room and adjoining kitchen. It was like camping out. Papa had cooked on his Coleman stove. Showers were put on hold to avoid freezing.

When it appeared reasonably certain that the power would not be restored any time soon they packed up for the motel, and Ben came home where the power had been back on line after only a day.

Ben and I walked outside the line of rooms on the upper level.

"Can we go in?" asked Ben.

"There's nobody here that we know," I said. "Sometime we'll stay here when Mom can come along."

Satisfied, Ben and I returned to the car. We drove back toward the entrance.

"There's a nice park," said Ben. "Let's go there."

So we parked the car and joined some other kids playing on the ladders and slides of the playground equipment. Ben was skilled at climbing and used the slide only as a necessary means to get to the bottom of the slide so he could climb up again.

I was relieved to see that the other kids were not obviously contagious. No runny noses or sneezing. I worried about Ben contracting a cold virus and developing another earache. I suffered from the worrisome vigilance of a parent for a child. I tried not to be too protective or worried, though it seemed to be an innate characteristic that I couldn't fully modify or control. I found this easier to do when someone was with us. I noticed the tension of another person and could ratchet my own anxiety down to a milder level.

"I need to go pee," announced Ben.

"I think there's a bathroom over there," I said pointing to the small building at the far end of the playground.

"What does it say?" asked Ben.

"The sign says 'closed for the season'," I said, a little perturbed.

"That's silly," said Ben, and of course it was.

"Maybe we can find a potty in the craft shop by the entrance," I said. We made our way back to the parking lot, and on to the craft shop.

"What's it say?" asked Ben.

"It says 'bathroom at the welcome center across the road'. Let's go there," I said.

We drove to the welcome center but it was closed.

"I tell you what," I said. "Let's go behind the trees, it's private."

When we finished, we went back to the craft shop.

"We could see if there's a gift for Mom," said Ben. Local crafts were displayed which made for fun browsing.

"Look at this, Tim," said Ben pointing to a bird house. "It's a school." The birdhouse was painted red with a black roof, the word 'school' had been painted over the hole.

"I want the birds to go to school, too," said Ben. "And I think Mom would like it. This can be her gift. Let's pay for it." And we did.

It was late afternoon when we drove home. Ben settled back leaning his head on the rest.

"Do you have any tapes we could play?" asked Ben.

I looked in the compartment, extracted a cassette and handed it to Ben.

"This might be a good one," he said.

"It's a Spanish language tape," I said after glancing at the cassette. "Do you want to listen to it?"

"Sure. What's Spanish?" he asked.

"It's a language, another way of talking. Here, you can listen," I said as I inserted the tape.

The announcer spoke a word in English then another voice said the word in its Spanish equivalent. It was quite soothing. Ben tried to repeat a few of the words. Then he leaned back and watched the scenery go by. In a few minutes, he slept. The tape played on as I drove down the state route.

I recalled that these roads were sometimes referred to as 'blue highways' and the pleasant thought of reading the book of the same title by William Least Heat Moon rose from the mists of my memory. For a dreamer, which I was, the thought was comforting.

I wondered if Ben retained any of the Spanish as he slept. He had repeated 'uno' when the voice on the tape pronounced it. Maybe just a coincidence or an association with the card game of the same name. The swirl of memories and associations filled my mind as I drove south toward home.

Ben displayed uncanny concentration and a memory to match, as demonstrated by his recollection of the ice storm when he was just two and a half years old. I tried to jog my own remembrance of things past but found the veils of time nearly impenetrable. My earliest memories were but memories of memories.

I remembered, as a teenager, remembering tales of deep snow through which I had trod to first grade when we lived in Emporia, Kansas. And from that same time, I recalled standing on the corner looking across the road to a building on the campus of Emporia State Teachers College (as it was then known) and seeing a darkened window on the top floor in which the older kids said ghosts lived. There were also memories of gathering acorns from the trees on the lawn of an apartment complex on our block to use for the great acorn wars; of the vacant lot across the street where my older playmates said Superman shot himself forcing the owner to subsequently raze the house for lack of anyone willing to buy such a blotted landmark; of the great newspaperman William Allen White writing about his daughter's untimely death; and more vague hints of my early life persisting in my memory.

I imagined Ben would be blessed with persistence of memory, too. And somehow this persistence would forge his character and personality, and offer him many opportunities to visit and then revisit his experiences on his journey from cradle to grave.

The memories of my youth took me back further to Lincoln, Nebraska, where I had been born in 1955. The Sand Hills of Nebraska covered about 20,000 square miles in the western part of the state. A journey there would take Ben and me through the state of my birth. We could easily dip down afterwards to Emporia to visit, for Ben, and revisit, for me. Experiencing the sandhill cranes swooping down to the broad Platte River banks and marshes might be unique enough to carve a niche in our memories and persist.

***

As the day approached for departure, we went over the checklist for the trip.

"The cranes are arriving," I said, "even as we speak."

"Well, you're not ready yet," said Janet. "So mind the business of getting ready. You know I'll be worried to death about you both. You can always change your mind, you know, you still have two days before you leave."

"We'll be ready," I said. "And you know I don't want you to worry. Even if you could take time off from work, you know you would never survive such a long car trip. You'd be sick half the time on some of the 'blue highways' we'll have to travel on. Besides, I can't turn back now. Ben has his heart set on seeing the cranes. Don't you Ben?"

"Sure. Can we see the cranes now, right now," said

Ben excitedly.

"Not right yet. We need some supplies from the store though. Can you ride along and help me?" I asked.

Janet sighed and managed a smile.

"Let's go," said Ben. At least Ben had no reservations.

On the way back from the store, where we bought snack food and juices, we drove past the usual houses and fields.

"Here, Tim, turn here," Ben shrieked excitedly.

I turned down a new subdivision road and on toward the end.

"What's down here, Ben?" I asked. "We're almost to the end. There's nothing down here except construction, and the road is gonna run out."

But to Ben the associations he made in his mind were becoming long-awaited reality.

"Yippee. Park over there," said Ben. "Can we get out and see it closer?"

As I moved the car to the designated spot, the object of Ben's excitement came into view from behind the last building under construction. It was a crane. A construction crane. And next to it was a large pile of sand.

"Sure, Ben," I said enlightened and somehow relieved. "Let's do that."

"I'm glad we get to see the sandhill crane," Ben said.

Nebraska, I realized, would have to wait for another season.

SPRING

Turn back, turn back, O time in thy flight. Make me a child again - Just for tonight.

-R.L. Stevenson
The Children's Hour

NO FOOLING
***

Another big day had arrived. Ben and I were up early.

"Let's fix pancakes," said Ben. I set out the Bisquick, eggs, milk, and bacon. Ben mixed the ingredients while I prepared the bacon.

"Something smells great," said Janet, joining us in the kitchen.

"It's bacon, Mom," said Ben. "And I'm fixing pancakes."

"Great," said Janet.

"You're up early," I said. "You can go back and rest a little longer."

"Oh, I feel fine. Let's eat," she said.

After breakfast, we dressed for a day of outdoor activities.

"Can I get 'Big Jake' today?" Ben asked.

Ben had been patient all week, a veritable eternity for his age, for the promised day when Janet would take him to get the riding battery powered dump truck.

"Yes, today is the day. You and Dad play outside while I finish getting ready," Janet said.

In the garage, Ben helped clean up and make room for the truck. We swept and loaded his Cozy Coupe, a red and yellow plastic toy riding car, into the back of my Pathfinder.

"Are you sure you can give this up," I asked as we loaded the Cozy Coupe.

Ben had agreed to give the Coupe to his cousin, along with a car seat and high chair which he no longer used. Ben had also agreed to give his FP1, a pedal powered three-wheeler, to the preschool at church and this he had done earlier in the week.

"Sure," said Ben.

"You guys have really cleaned this place up. It looks great," said Janet. I had moved boxes and boards around and the garage looked spacious.

"Let's go now," Ben said.

We loaded up and buckled up. After backing out, Janet pressed the garage door remote. The door descended and stopped with a metal crunching thud.

"What was that?" she asked. She pushed the remote button again, and another crunch. I was ashen.

"Oh no, I know what it is," I said as I frantically tried to open the car door. "Can you come around and open my door, the child safety lock is on."

"So what's wrong with the garage door?" Janet asked as she opened the car door.

I opened the garage, angry with myself, and pointed to a wooden box I had placed too close to the side support in the garage. The box had been ripped down the edge next to the garage door. I examined the rest of the door. The metal door had buckled and bent. I took a deep breath and exhaled.

"You two should go on. I'll have to try to fix the door," I said.

"You stay, we'll go," said Janet.

"You come too, Tim," Ben said.

"Dad can't come now Ben, he's got work to do," Janet said. "I'll call later. Good luck." They drove away.

"Thanks," I said. And I knew I would need it.

I began the process of taking apart the garage door. Screws, nuts, struts all came off. Then - a glitch. Two screws were stuck fast. I tried oil and hammer taps to loosen them up. Wouldn't budge. Stop and think. The telephone number of the door company taunted me.

"I can do this myself," I said to myself.

Reluctantly, I called the company's number. No answer. I would have to do the repairs myself. I needed a socket wrench for the right torque.

The telephone rang. Janet and Ben were at Aunt Bess' house. I told of the progress and the impasse.

"Hold on," said Janet. In a minute, she was back on the line. "They have a set of socket wrenches here. We'll bring them by."

To pass the time, I decided to fold the laundry and remake the bed. I felt as if I were making the best of a trying situation and it kept my thoughts away from the damage I had done to the door. Clothes folded and put away, bed remade.

Then I saw the spots on the carpet.

"Oh no," I moaned. "What now?" I inspected the

spots more closely and realized I had tracked grease all over the house. I sighed. Then I located the stain remover from the pantry and went to work again. Most of the spots resolved. It would take more work later. A hapless giddiness overwhelmed me. I would make a run for it before they returned, and hide, maybe stay holed up somewhere until this run of luck ended. Then I could return. Maybe Janet would take me back.

Meanwhile, Janet and Ben arrived home with the socket wrenches.

"Your car is possessed," she said. "The alarm goes off everytime I get in or out. It's scaring us."

"You have to use the remote device every time," I explained.

"Well, here are your wrenches. We're heading out to get the dump truck," she said. I told her about the stains. She said we could work on them later.

The socket wrenches worked. I had everything disassembled and pounded into shape when they returned at dusk.

"I'm ready to put it all back together," I announced.

We all took a break to eat and discuss the door, spots, possessed car, and the dump truck.

"Can I ride it now," asked Ben.

"First it has to charge overnight but you can help me finish the garage project," I said.

Ben and I worked in the garage until bedtime. Miraculously the door was reassembled and no permanent damage remained. The dump truck was charging and would be ready for use tomorrow early. Janet had attacked the spots and the carpet looked fine.

Later, Janet took Ben to his room for bedtime stories. I reviewed my repairs and went to the bathroom to clean up. In the adjacent closet I hung up some of Janet's clothes from the day's laundry. I discovered I had dried her new all cotton pants and they had shrunk. I should have made a run for it earlier when I had a chance. Maybe she wouldn't notice. Naw, she noticed everything.

I went to the kitchen for a cup of tea.

"Tomorrow has got to be a better day," I told myself.

I looked at the schedule on which I wrote my daily chores. That confirmed it would be a better day. Afterall, tomorrow would be April 2nd.

***

SPRING FEVER

***

The lilacs smelled pungent in the warm breeze. Irises elevated their buds to the sun. Peonies would bloom soon, too. Daylight savings time had wreaked its havoc on sleeping schedules and there was little to do but 'spring forward' and adjust, usually just in time to 'fall back' in the fall.

"Am I forty pounds?" asked Ben. He looked forward to achieving this plateau for he knew it meant he no longer had to use the car seat.

"Let's try the scale," I said.

"What's it say?" asked Ben.

"Thirty-eight and a half," I said.

"Is that forty?" said Ben.

"Almost," I said.

Later, outside, we played on Ben's collection of riding vehicles. I watched as he sped down the driveway then slammed on the brakes to skid the rear wheels forward bringing the rear end of the Big Jake dump truck sliding sideways and even with the front wheels. Frisky, I thought. Must be the weather. Middle Tennessee was made all the more delightful during the mild spring months and it was evident in the play of the kids, young and old.

Ben circled the cul-du-sac and headed up the long grade of the driveway.

"I need motor assist," he yelled to me. I walked down to give Ben a push. Ben whopped me accidently as he swung his hand around to call for more power.

"Push harder, lazybones," said Ben.

"Be careful, Ben, you coulda hurt me." I rubbed my jaw.

At the top of the drive, I knelt down to talk to Ben. It must have been the weather. Ben backhanded me.

Remain calm, don't scream, I reminded myself.

"You can't hit people, Ben."

Ben started to do it again. I backed away. Then I picked him up.

"You'll just have to have a little quiet time," I said as I carried Ben to the garage.

Inside, I realized I couldn't hold Ben as he struggled without one or both of us coming out the worse for it. I opened the car door and put Ben in his car seat and fastened it.

"Ben, you'll have to stay here 'til you calm down," I said. And, I thought, until I calm down, too.

I stood nearby with the door open and quietly waited. Ben kept demanding to get out or to stay in with the door closed. Whenever I tried to suggest something, Ben wanted the opposite. So we sat there and sat there. Until Ben spent himself and became quiet.

Discipline is unpleasant, I thought, but sometimes you have to try medicine even if it's just spring fever you're trying to cure.

NOT IN OUR WORLD
***

"What are you typing?" asked Ben.

The computer screen glowed blue.

"I'm gonna type a story. What kind of stories do you like?" I asked.

"I like Jack and the Beanstalk," said Ben.

"That's a good one," I said. We recited the known facts of the story and then Ben added some modifications.

"The giant is really good. Sometimes he's good and bad," said Ben.

"Is Jack scared of the giant?" I asked.

"Not too much," said Ben.

"How do you make the giant good?" I asked. Ben thought.

"You give him food and play with him."

"That's a good idea. Then he's not hungry and he's happy," I said.

"That's right," said Ben.

"You'd have to have a big place to play with a giant," I said. "Maybe you could play in the giant's house."

"Sure," said Ben. "There's lots of room. The giant's really good, but not the other giants."

"How many are there?" I asked.

"Lots of 'em," said Ben.

"That is a good story. I like it too," I said. We

talked about other stories we liked, and the characters in those stories.

"Do they live in our world?" asked Ben.

"Not really. They live in books and videos, and in our minds," I said.

I recalled my amusement, many years ago, when Ben's cousin Tony had said he wished his comic book superheroes were real. Ben seemed content that at least some of the imaginary characters and creatures were not real, or at least not in our world.

***

TWINKLE

***

Janet and Ben paged through the album.

"Was I just a twinkle in your eye?" asked Ben.

"Yes, you were." Janet smiled.

They looked at the pictures and talked about everybody in our wedding. Ben mistook his cousin Katie for her younger sister Lyndy. This was understandable since at the time of our marriage Katie was Lyndy's age now.

"Can I be in your wedding?" Ben's moist eyes met his mom's as he softly pleaded.

There aren't many times when a look or word touches you in such a way that life seems infinite and unfathomable. This may not have been such a time, but if it wasn't then it was an honorable mention.

As Janet hesitated, not knowing quite how to respond, Ben got up and walked over to the cabinet. He picked up a framed picture of himself and returned to his mom.

"Put this in the book," he said. "Then I'll be in the wedding."

***

TRACTORS

***

"I just like to mow my grass myself," said Ben.

And so we drove to the store that sold John Deere lawnmowers. An ad had run on the local cable station. The store was having a promotional contest to give away a STX 38. Shiny green paint, simple controls.

"I can sit on your lap," said Ben. "I'll drive and you can use the brake."

Comments of neighbors cast doubt on the length of interest in lawnmowers. They believed the affection would fade by the time Ben entered his teenage years. Voices of experience? Time would provide the answer.

Uncertain where the store was located we drove along several roads. As if destiny was our guide, we found the place after only one errant detour.

"Ah, beautiful," said Ben.

And they were. Even better looking than the picture on television. It had rained and most of the seats were still wet. A salesman wiped one for Ben to try. He wanted to take one home which required an explanation of the workings of the contest.

"Let's enter then," said Ben. Inside the showroom were more tractors on display. While Ben and Janet looked around, I found the entry box and stuffed it with entry forms. Ben came over to help.

"I feel lucky," he said. Janet and I agreed he was lucky, which he needed to be to win.

"Can I take the tractor home now?" asked Ben.

"Not 'til June 1st. And only if we win," said Janet.

"They'll draw one entry out of this box and if it's ours they'll call us to come down and pick it up," I added.

"How can we pick it up?" asked Ben.

"Maybe we'll borrow a truck," I said.

"Or maybe they'll deliver," said Janet.

We looked around the showroom some more. This place was ready for kids. Toy tractors were available for sale. Ben handled several but he wasn't interested in buying any today. He had his mind on winning the big riding mower.

As it turned out, Ben didn't win the mower but his enthusiasm remained undiminished for powerful machines. He started saving his money for a mower. He liked Uncle Bro's Kubota and Papa's Dynamark and he even mentioned he wanted to be a Bobcat operator when he grew up.

"When I get big and you get little you can sit on my lap," he explained. "When will I get big?"

And before I could answer, Ben sensed the answer and fired the follow up.

"Why does it take so long?"

***

GARDENING REVISITED

***

"I got grass seeds germinating outside in a pot," announced Ben proudly to Janet.

Ben and I had played in the garden most of the afternoon. I planted petunias and verbena while Ben dug a half-foot square of soil and filled it with grass. Ben placed a pot over the soil.

"That's so the lawnmower man doesn't run over it," he said. He had a long term outlook for a three-year-old.

A week earlier, in a neighbor's backyard, Ben watched as a dozen dumptruck loads of dirt were delivered and smoothed around by a Bobcat, a small loader. Of course, he wanted a Bobcat for his own use.

Seeds were scattered over the dirt and then a layer of straw. The neighbor explained that the seeds would take a week or two to germinate. Janet and Ben talked about germination frequently during the next week.

Every day Ben journeyed over to the neighbor's yard to view the straw-covered area.

"Have the seeds germinated yet?" he asked.

About a week later, the first green sprouts appeared. And daily afterwards, more and more grass poked through the straw cover.

Ben was impressed that something grew from an apparent nothingness. But he understood that the seeds were the beginning point and that they changed into grass. Germination was the name of the magic that he witnessed. It was natural for him to use the word and use the word correctly, though it surprised me to hear Ben speak the word so casually.

The next morning I rousted Ben out of bed.

"When do things die?" Ben sat up and asked.

Ben didn't seem worried just curious. I was taken aback. I tried to remember what Mr. Rogers said when Mr. McFeely brought that dead bird on the television show. And, too, I thought of Nathan fighting the brain tumor.

I tried to think of a safe answer. Should I say when they get old or sick? I dismissed this response because Ben had been sick and didn't die, and Ben knew that most people were older than he was and they hadn't died. Something else was needed but I wasn't ready with an answer because I hadn't thought much about the question.

"When they decide they can't live anymore, I guess," I said. I felt like a bozo. "Of course, you don't need to worry 'cause you like to play and have fun, right?"

"Yes, I do and I like to play and play," said Ben.

"When do you think things die?" I asked.

With carefree ease and confidence, Ben answered me.

"When they don't germinate."

***

FLIGHT OF FANCY

***

"I'm using my imagination," said Ben. "Does that make it come true?"

"Well, that's a start," I said. "Then you have to do something like building or playing to make it come true." The response occurred to me suddenly and there I had said it. I felt some discussion would be useful.

"Just because you imagine something doesn't make it come true. For example, if you imagine monsters that won't make them appear." I wanted to cover the downside first before progressing to the brighter, lighter side.

"I'm using my imagination to fly in an airplane when I grow up," said Ben.

He had practiced flying airplanes often. Of course he pretended to be a builder, landscaper, gardener, police officer, recycler, and a myriad of other occupations depending on his daily or weekly focus.

"Can I fly an airplane when I grow up?" Ben asked.

"Sure," I said.

"That's right," said Ben. "And I can fly to Nanny and Papa's house while you drive the car. Or I can fly to Cincinnati to see Mammie."

"Maybe, I can fly with you," I said.

"That's a good idea," Ben beamed. "And I'll stop at the stoplights."

"When you fly there aren't any stoplights," I smiled. "You'll be much higher than the roads and lights. But you can stop if you want to."

"No, I'll just fly way up in the sky," said Ben. "And I'll use my compass, and my headphones."

Ben knew about such things from Papa. Papa had built Ben his first airplane. It was about six feet long and had a wing span of about seven feet. When the use and weather deteriorated it too much, we discarded it and Papa built a bigger two-seater, about twelve feet long with a wing span of about sixteen feet. This model they used when Ben visited their home, and they took long journeys with the propeller whirring and headphones in place to talk to the tower.

Now Papa was in the midst of his great airplane project. In his garage he worked on a honest-to-goodness airplane.

"When can I fly in an airplane?" asked Ben.

"Well, Papa is building a real plane and when it's finished you can fly it," I said.

"But when will it be finished?" he asked.

"It's a big project, it'll take about a year. Maybe when you're five or six you can fly it," I said.

"Maybe when I'm Lyndy's age I can fly it," said Ben. His cousin Lyndy was six. Time, too, was a relative.

***

COMPANIONSHIP

***

"I wish I had a brother," said Ben. He was busy loading holly clippings into his Big Jake for hauling to a mulch pile. Ben wore his work gloves to protect his hands from the prickly points on the holly leaves. We had used the hedge trimmer together to trim the bush and now jointly cleaned the site.

"Mom and I think we're mighty lucky just to have you, Ben. I think you're great," I said.

"If I had a brother, he could operate the Big Jake and I could put a load into the dumptruck," said Ben as he drove off to deliver another load.

"If we had another brother, you know, he would be small, like your cousin Jake," I said. Jake was six months old.

"Why would he be small?" asked Ben.

"That's how everybody starts out. Then they grow up," I said, "It would take a few years before he could help load."

Ben thought about the explanation.

"That's okay if he's small like Jake," he said.

I tried my best to be a buddy to Ben but this only reenforced what I knew - that it just wasn't the same.

***

MOONBEAMS

***

"The moon is moving," said Ben as he drove his Big
Jake down the road. He watched the reflective ball as it
seemingly followed his movements.

"Now it's stopped," he said as he stopped. And he
looked at me quizzically.

"I don't think it's following you. It just seems to move
when you move," I said.

I hesitated to say that it's not really moving. I had told
Ben many times that the moon moves around the Earth.
Ben didn't seem interested in the technical explanation, he
enjoyed making the moon move when he moved. During
the sunny days, warm or cold, he drove with purpose.
Fortunately, the speed was a comfortable walking pace and
I kept up without fatigue.

"Let's catch some animals," said Ben.

Ben transposed characters and stories from video and
book to his real life adventures. He could be Bernard, the
mouse in the Walt Disney film *The Rescuers*, or Robin
Hood, or Moglie from *The Jungle Book*, while I played the
role of the close friend and helper. When Ben was Bernard
I was the Albatross; when Ben was Robin, I was Little
John; when Ben was Moglie, I was Baloo the bear.
Eventually, everybody in the family was assigned roles to
play but Ben maintained his position of the hero. Except

on this day, Ben wanted to be Mcleish, the bad guy in *The Rescuers*.

"Who can I be?" I asked.

"You be Joanna," said Ben. Joanna was the companion, a lizard.

"We'll catch animals and put them in the bushwacker," he continued.

We went along and went along until Ben spotted the first specimen.

"This is a kangaroo," said Ben picking a dandelion. "I'll put it in my bushwacker." Ben placed the weed in the back of the truck.

"Here's another," I said. I picked a white dandelion and showed Ben how to blow the seeds all off. Ben liked doing that and tried another.

"We need to find some eagle eggs," said Ben. He drove further down the road to a neighbor's driveway and down the drive to the gravel pile in the back.

"These are eagle eggs, Joanna," he said. We collected a few rocks and added them to the collection. Then we headed for the house, stopping to gather more specimens along the way.

"The moon's following me again," said Ben.

It was a sight worthy of note. It was one of those rare days when the sun was low in the west but not on the horizon and the waxing moon rose in the east.

"How can we get the moon?" Ben asked. I was stumped.

"We can probably catch it in a tree," said Ben. He stopped his truck when he had positioned a tree between it and the moon.

"Let's climb the tree and get it out," Ben said.

"Are you talking about the moon?" I asked.

"I'm talking about the moon," Ben affirmed.

"Lift me up," Ben said, approaching the tree.

I lifted him to the closest limb.

"Now you climb up too," said Ben.

I swung his leg over a perpendicular limb. We sat there, a few feet off the ground while Ben studied the situation. "There's a problem," Ben said.

"What's the problem?" I asked.

"I don't think this will work," said Ben.

"What should we do?" I said.

Ben examined the bark.

"Here's an ant. That's funny."

The ant crawled over the ridges and grooves of the bark. Ben put his finger near the ant.

"Will it get me?"

"Naw, it's okay," I said.

"Let's smush it," said Ben.

"Oh, no need to do that," I said. "It won't hurt us. It's probably looking for something to eat."

"I'm ready to get down now," said Ben.

We climbed down. I got down first and lifted Ben off the limb and swung him to the ground. Ben got back in his truck and drove across the yard.

"Swing me," he said.

I buckled him in the swing and pushed.

"Higher, please," said Ben happily. The swing went higher and higher as I pushed. The ropes were attached to a huge oak limb some thirty feet above the ground.

"I can reach it," said Ben. With one hand Ben held the rope and with the other he grabbed at something in the air.

"Hold on," I said.

"Higher, higher," yelled Ben.

"What can you reach?" I said.

Ben didn't answer. His concentration was acute. The arc of the swing was wildly precarious.

"Hold on or I'll have to stop," I yelled.

Ben was oblivious. He was flying.

"More, more."

And then he lifted his other hand and stretched both straight out. The swing lurched for equilibrium. I gulped as my heart rose into my throat.

"I got it!" said Ben and brought his hands back to hold the rope. And I saw the object of Ben's efforts and got it too.

"The moon," said Ben. "I touched the moon."

The sun and the moon smiled down on the big oak tree where Ben and I were suspended in our world, swinging up and down and up.

***

THREE NO MORE
***

Ben had been asleep for about thirty minutes when he cried out. I went to his bedside.

"What's wrong, buddy?" I asked as I rubbed his brow.

"I woke up because I thought I heard Nanny," Ben said.

"Did you have a dream?"

"Yes. Nanny was in my heart," Ben spoke calmly, a little drowsy.

"What did she say?" I asked.

Ben yawned and smiled.

"Have a good day."

I hummed a song for Ben until we both were quiet and Ben seemed to be asleep.

"Good night," I whispered as I quietly walked to the door.

"I like your singing," Ben said as I closed the door.

And that was the last I heard as I walked through the doorway and the last I would hear from my three-year-old boy as he lay on the bottom bunk tucked in for the night.

For tomorrow, when he woke, he'd be four and the conversations with a three-year-old would be no more.

***

EPILOGUE
(For Nathan)

***

You know how much you miss something by how hard you try to get it back after it's gone. On days like this I believe strongly that we all try to recapture lost times, to grasp them and not let go. But in the end, you have to let go to go on.

Ben has had his fourth birthday. He has begun another year of school, another precious year of life.

Autumn has come again.

Outside the rains drag down the weakest of leaves. Their carnage litters the ground, evidence of the rage during the darkest hours. Last night a great battle was fought between the warmth struggling to give the living a few minutes more of life but inevitably the heavier, colder north winds prevailed and left a killing frost on which the leaves now lie. I know the patterns of birth and death but that offers little comfort now. Time marches on relentlessly.

I shuffle numbly to the window trying hard to get something back. I touch the reflection of my face and it confirms the cold smooth glassiness but nothing more. The light bouncing off the pane conjures up a smiling face in a photograph I once held. The boy in the photo was not quite four years old. His name was Nathan. Straining my eyes the image becomes palpable. Nathan is smiling, giddy, as he poses with his heroes at Disneyworld. I scan my mystic image for clues. Other than the hairless scalp I detect none. I can't see inside his head, but his heart exudes joy and that I can make out. I can't see the faces of Mickey Mouse or Goofy clearly. I have seen many pictures of them. They all merge. They are always smiling anyway, and in my heart I am glad that they do and always will. But it is the boy's face that holds me transfixed. He radiates such good feelings toward the camera or maybe it's to his parents who are with him. And since this is a photograph, he always will.

Rain thumps on my window pane and the image vanishes, but it is replaced by another. In the distance I watch a line of geese undulate with the wind currents southward. Nathan loved ducks and geese, those that habitated the pond near his home. His mother helped him cut up a loaf of bread. Nathan was allowed to use a dull butter knife which was nearly as useless on the bread as the razor sharp surgeon scalpels were on his tumor. That which he could not cut he tore into small pieces so the geese and ducks wouldn't have to struggle swallowing. Nathan was thoughtful by experience. The bread was stuffed skillfully back into the bag by the not quite four-year-old hands.

When their car drove into the parking lot by the pond, one duck approached as if in recognition. Nathan nearly leapt from the car to get to his ducks. The wild cacophony which arose from this mutual nourishing echoed across the life sustaining waters. When the bread was depleted Nathan pleaded with his mother for more. They made three successive trips that day. Nathan feeding his ducks, and they somehow nourishing him. Maybe it was their wildness, their freedom, their flight that he wanted to merge with.

Later that evening, his mother held Nathan closer than ever before, giving him a few minutes more of her strength, as she read to him from his favorite story book. He was tired, his frail body nearly limp, but not so much that he couldn't give his mother one more smile, one more kiss on the cheek, one more snuggle before he closed his eyes. Before his warmth succumbed to the relentless north wind of time marching on.

Maybe he dreamt of the ducks taking bread, honking, taking flight. Maybe he flew with them. Higher and lighter than he had ever gone before.

At least that is my hope for Nathan, as I watch my reflection blur in my window pane.

***

The End

ACKNOWLEDGEMENTS

Thanks to Janet for her encouragement and support. Thanks to Ben for the conversations. And to Nanny and Papa, and my family for the love of storytelling. Thanks also to Angie for editing the entire manuscript.

I am grateful also to the influence of Art Linkletter (kids do say the darnedest things), Captain Kangaroo, and Fred Rogers (and the neighborhood).

I have many others to acknowledge. Some here, some privately. This book's title is a variation of the name of the fine play by Robert Bolt about Thomas More. Janet, my wife, was graduated from Thomas More College. My son's godfather carries the name, Thomas More. That's more than enough *coincidence* for me.

ABOUT THE AUTHOR

Tim Wibking lives near Franklin, Tennessee with his wife and son. They are currently trying to adopt a child from China. He is working on his next book about China's children.